by Dave Godfrey

Visit the *Seaside Rock* website: www.scriptureunion.org.uk/seasiderock

Access downloadable versions of the drama scripts and music score for the memory verse songs plus other resources.

Share your experiences on the bulletin board and get advice from others.

Register for *Seaside Rock* to:

☀ Discover who's running *Seaside Rock* in your area

☀ Help other churches run *Seaside Rock*

☀ Receive information from SU about other relevant resources.

Scripture Union, 207–209 Queensway, Bletchley, Milton Keynes MK2 2EB, England.

© Dave Godfrey, 2003.

ISBN 1 85999 498 9

British Library Cataloguing-in-Publication Data
A catalogue record for this book is available from the British Library.

Scripture quotations taken from the Contemporary English Version © American Bible Society, 1991, 1992, 1995. Anglicisations © British and Foreign Bible Society 1996. Published in the UK by HarperCollins*Publishers* and used with permission.

Printed and bound by Interprint Ltd, Malta

Cover illustration by Colin Smithson
Cover design by FourNineZero
Internal design by FourNineZero
Beach Lookout artwork by Paula Langdon

Seaside Rock CD
Programming and production: Matt Osgood
Guitar: Mark Currey
Vocals: Dave Godfrey, Rachel Lindley, Matt Osgood

Scripture Union is an international Christian charity working with churches in more than 130 countries providing resources to bring the good news about Jesus Christ to children, young people and families – and to encourage them to develop spiritually through the Bible and prayer.

As well as our network of volunteers, staff and associates who run holidays, church-based events and school Christian groups, we produce a wide range of publications and support those who use our resources through training programmes.

For Menna, Timothy, Anna and Esther.

For the children of the Gladiators Club,
the SU Invaders Holiday and the Earlston *Seaside Rock* holiday club
who helped develop the ideas contained within this book.

Keep following Jesus – the living Rock!

Dave Godfrey, March 2002

Dave Godfrey is an experienced primary teacher and children's worker. He leads a weekly outreach children's club in York, a bimonthly city-wide Praise Party and an extensive training programme on behalf of the York Schools and Youth Trust. He now spends the majority of his time with his own organisation, Omega Zone Ministries, travelling to lead Praise Party events for children, and training those who work with children. Dave is a Spring Harvest 8–11s leader, and a songwriter.

Dave Godfrey has recorded the following CDs of his own music for children:

Brave and Daring
CD/Tape/Songbook

Shoulders of Giants
CD/Songbook and CD/Full Teachers Pack

Heaven's No.1
CD/Tape/Songbook and Backing Track CD

Dependence Day
CD/Tape/Songbook & Backing Track CD

Seaside Rock Single

This CD contains the **Seaside Rock** theme song, Memory Verse medley (both taken from the cover CD) and *Ace Foundations* (taken from *Heaven's No. 1*) and is an ideal take-home gift at the end of a **Seaside Rock** holiday club.

To purchase copies of the **Seaside Rock** CD single, or any of Dave's albums, or for further information on his ministry, contact Dave on:

Omega Zone Ministries

PO Box 94, Copmanthorpe, York, YO23 3WW
T: 01904 778848 E: Dave@omegazone.org.uk Website: www.omegazone.org.uk

CNTENTS

PART 1 — What is *Seaside Rock*?

The sun is out, the sky is blue, *Seaside Rock* is just for you!

Seaside Rock is a five-day children's holiday club programme. It is packed with creative teaching, games, songs, Bible focus, prayers and craft ideas, along with a drama script for each day. *Seaside Rock* provides a mixture of small group activities and presentation from the front. The material includes two family services – one designed to launch a holiday club and the other to round it off. Alternatively, these could be used to extend the programme to seven days.

Seaside Rock is written for use with children between the ages of five and eleven, and is fast-moving, creative and fun, with a strong teaching element to it.

Holiday clubs can be special times. Children can meet Jesus and have a great time as they do so. I challenge you to go down to the seaside for a week of high-impact children's ministry!

Dave Godfrey

Dave Godfrey

THE AIMS OF *SEASIDE ROCK*

Seaside Rock is based around the story of Peter. *Seaside Rock* will:

- ☀ introduce children to Jesus through the stories and experiences of Peter.
- ☀ encourage children to build their lives on Jesus the Rock.
- ☀ provide a fast-moving, fun and action-packed holiday club programme.

THEME AND SETTING

Seaside Rock, as the name suggests, is set at the seaside. Your venue will be transformed into a seaside setting, complete with sand, sea and a seaside house that is built on rock. The rock theme is picked up in different ways:

☀ The drama for the week is based around the parable of the wise and foolish builders.

☀ Peter, the Rock, tells the children what life was really like with Jesus, either through using the *Seaside Rock* video, or by Peter's live appearance!

☀ Through the *Seaside Rock* theme song, seaside games and activities.

SEASIDE ROCK TERMINOLOGY

The Lifeguard
The main presenter of the *Seaside Rock* holiday club

The Rock Band
The music group

Rock Groups
The small groups that the children will be part of

Rock Group leader
Leader of a Rock Group

Rock Pools
Where the Rock Groups meet

Beach Lookout
An updated version of 'Kim's Game' played every day

In for a Swim!
The games and craft ideas

Lyn the Bin
A leader dressed up as a dustbin who presents the children's comments and jokes every day.

Heather on the Weather
A leader who does a short spoof weather forecast every day.

THE *SEASIDE ROCK* VIDEO

The *Seaside Rock* video contains five episodes with Peter down at the seaside telling the stories of Jesus. A *Seaside Rock* leader needs to summarise the main points and challenge children to make an appropriate response.

TEACHING PROGRAMME

Peter was an amazing man and the New Testament is full of stories about him, as well as containing some of his writings. He was kind-hearted, quick, forceful, hopeful, impulsive and a man of extremes. Peter wore his heart on his sleeve – it got him into trouble at times, but it also brought the praise of Jesus. He was the first of the disciples to pronounce that Jesus was the Messiah, yet, when Peter challenged his path to the cross, Jesus had to say to him, 'Get behind me, Satan!'

During this week we'll follow the highs and lows of Peter's friendship with Jesus. Each story points to Jesus as the Saviour and the source of Peter's hope and joy. The most important section of *Seaside Rock* is its teaching programme. It should be well planned, prayed through, prepared and presented clearly. The programme will challenge the children to follow Jesus, just as Peter did two thousand years ago.

More details of Peter's life and ministry can be found on page 78.

	PETER	KEY STORY	KEY LINK TO THE HOLIDAY CLUB	KEY PASSAGE
FAMILY SERVICE A Sunday before the club		Andrew brings Peter to Jesus, an act that changed his life!	This week we will bring children to Jesus, and children will bring their friends to Jesus.	John 1:35–42
DAY 1 Peter, the Rock	Peter introduces himself as Simon. He tells how Jesus called him to follow.	Jesus calls Peter. Peter's testimony.	Jesus loves everyone, even tough people like Peter.	Luke 5:1–11 Matthew 16:13–20
DAY 2 The wise and foolish builders Peter walking on the water	Peter retells the story of the wise and foolish builders outlining Jesus' practical teaching about anger and bad words.	The wise and foolish builders. Peter's experience of walking on water is tied in to this parable.	Jesus wants us to listen to him and obey.	Matthew 7:24–27; 14:22–32.
DAY 3 Jesus heals Peter's mother-in-law	Peter tells how Jesus came to his house to see his mother-in-law and healed her. (Plus one or two other miracles that convince him of who Jesus is.)	The healing of Peter's mother-in-law	Jesus is powerful and he is interested in ordinary families.	Matthew 8:14,15.
DAY 4 Peter and the Cross	Peter tells of his denial and Jesus' crucifixion using the symbols of bread and wine, how he really let Jesus down, and how Jesus died to forgive him!	Peter's denial and Jesus' crucifixion	Like Peter, we mess things up. Jesus died to put things right between us and God.	Matthew 26:17–35 58,69–75.
DAY 5 The Rock that lives	Peter tells of Jesus' resurrection, and how Jesus forgave him on the beach. Jesus warns of persecution, and encourages us with his words that Jesus is the Rock that lives.	Breakfast on the beach. Peter's words about Jesus the living Rock.	Jesus is alive today, and wants us to follow him, even when others think we are mad, and pick on us!	John 21:1–19 1 Peter 2:4–8
FAMILY SERVICE B After the club	Peter heals the lame man.	Peter and John heal the lame man,	We too need to share the good news with others.	Acts 3:1–10

7

A SUGGESTED DAILY PROGRAMME FOR *SEASIDE ROCK*

Suggested length of club: $2^1/_4$ hours (plus $1^1/_4$ hours team time)
(The material is flexible and can be adapted to fit into a reduced or an extended amount of time.)

9:00 – 9:30 (30 minutes)	**TEAM PREPARATION AND PRAYER**	
9:30 – 9:40 (10 minutes)	**ROCK POOL WELCOME**	Rock Pool group time
9:40 – 10:15 (35 minutes)	**WELCOME TO THE SEASIDE!**	Heather on the Weather Dancing on the Beach Beach Lookout Theme song Peter's story – retold live or on video Teaching Application Holiday Snapshots: memory verse
10:15 – 10:25 (10 minutes)	**ROCK POOL CHALLENGE**	Short activity and Bible discussion, centred on the day's theme (choose between a number of activities suggested for each day)
10:25 – 10:30 (5 minutes)	**REFRESHMENT KIOSK**	Refreshments as the children go to activities
10:30 – 10:55 (25 minutes)	**IN FOR A SWIM!**	Beach Games and Beach Craft
10:55 – 11:35 (40 minutes)	**LET'S GO SUNBATHE!**	Mega Question on the screen – reinforcing the day's teaching Songs Lyn the Bin Memory jogger Drama Creative prayer Theme song
11:35 – 11:45 (10 minutes)	**ROCK POOL GROUPS**	Collect belongings, receive *Seaside Rock* daily postcard, depart
11:45 – 12:30 (45 minutes)	**TEAM TIME**	Tidying up, team debrief and preparation for the following day

PROGRAMME BREAKDOWN

Each day's programme contains the following elements:

BACKGROUND NOTES

Aims

The main aims for the day

Team preparation

Notes to help you prepare for the day, including:

 *Bible reading and study*

This has two purposes. Firstly, to ensure that the leaders are familiar with the topics and teaching for the day, and secondly to provide a chance for the team to study the Bible for themselves, not just as teachers, but in a more personal, devotional way.

 Prayer

Final encouragements and practical preparations for the day

Equipment checklist

A useful way of checking that all the resources are ready for the day.

SESSION CONTENT

ROCK POOL WELCOME (10 minutes)

When the children arrive at *Seaside Rock*, they register and go straight into their Rock Groups. During this group time, the key aims will be team building and feedback. On Days 2–5, this is an excellent opportunity to check out who can remember the memory verse from the previous day. This short ten-minute section allows for late arrivals to join the group before going down to the seaside. Any children bringing pictures or jokes for Lyn the Bin should put them in Lyn's bin as they arrive.

WELCOME TO THE SEASIDE! (25 minutes)

This section of the programme is designed to be fast moving and fun. It contains the main teaching for the day and other elements outlined below. More details can be found in the Ideas bank on page 41. During this time, the children are all together for activities led from the front. It includes:

Dancing on the Beach

This is an aerobic workout. It gives the children a chance to stretch their muscles in a fun way. It can include simple exercises, but it can be made exciting by using fun actions which fit in with the seaside or teaching themes. This should be set to fast, lively music. Be aware of any children with disabilities. For example, if you have a child in a wheelchair, include lots of hand actions.

Beach Lookout

This is a team version of Kim's Game. Show the children a set of pictures which all link into the day's theme. There is a prepared set of pictures for each day to photocopy with each day's programme. The children have thirty seconds to look at the pictures, before the OHP is turned off. They then have ninety seconds as a Rock Group to try and call out as many things as they can remember, with a leader writing a list of the group's answers. The Lifeguard then reveals the pictures one by one, with the Rock Group leaders marking their team's sheet. Award points for correct answers. If no point system is in operation, declare the team with the most correct answers 'Beach Lookout daily champions'. See the *Seaside Rock* website for some ideas for running a points system through the week.

Singing

Children enjoy singing and learning new songs. See page 27 for the *Seaside Rock* theme song. You may wish to use the holiday club as an opportunity to learn new songs.

Peter's story – live or on video

The most important part of the morning is the teaching section, during which we meet Peter the Rock, and discover how his life changed by meeting Jesus. This could either happen by showing the children the relevant episode from the *Seaside Rock* video, or by a 'live' visit from Peter. A script for Peter can be found in each day's programme.

Teaching application

The Lifeguard should take the main points of Peter's story and help the children to apply them to their own lives (see each day's programme).

Holiday Snapshots

See page 25 for some creative ideas on how to use memory verses, including information on the memory verse song for each day. The words of the memory verse song are a paraphrase. The *Seaside Rock* CD contains all the songs.

ROCK POOL CHALLENGE (10 minutes)

Each day the children will take part in a short activity/Bible discussion, designed to reinforce their learning. This will be introduced by the Lifeguard from the front, and led in groups by the Rock Group leaders. You will need marker pens, large sheets of flip chart paper and copies of the Bible passage. As the Rock Group is where children read the Bible together, it should not be an optional extra.

REFRESHMENT KIOSK (5 minutes)

Be creative in providing refreshments. Try making shaped biscuits (starfish, seahorses, fish, etc.) or rock cakes. Or give out shrimp sweets and serve your drinks with colourful straws. You might even be able to get hold of a candy floss machine. Be aware of any allergies. On the last day, you might wish to give each child an ice lolly.

IN FOR A SWIM! (25 minutes)

Groups go to their Beach Games and Beach Craft activities.

LET'S GO SUNBATHE! (40 minutes)

During this period of time the children are all together for activities led from the front. It includes:

Mega Question

As the different groups return from their various activities, put an acetate on the OHP with a key question that focuses the children's thoughts back to the main teaching point of the day (see Beach Lookout page in each day's programme). This should be discussed in groups, and the Lifeguard should take a few answers from children/leaders before restating the main teaching point made earlier in the day.

Song/Memory jogger

This is a good opportunity to go back over the memory verse tackled earlier in the morning. You could also sing a song or two, depending on how much time is available.

Lyn the Bin

Lyn's job is to read out some of the jokes and show some of the pictures that the children have put in her dustbin when they arrived at *Seaside Rock*.

Seaside Rock drama

Follow the story of Chris and Phil in their efforts to build the Golden Palace.

Creative prayer

At the end of each day's programme is a creative prayer idea, which everyone can take part in and enjoy.

Theme song

It's always good to finish with a song. This could be the *Seaside Rock* theme song. Full and backing track recordings can be found on the *Seaside Rock* CD.

ROCK POOL GROUPS (5 minutes)

Each day the children will be given a *Seaside Rock* postcard, which includes the day's memory verse. These are not designed for use during the club time – they are for the children to take home and do on their own or with their family. They are a means of building a bridge between the church and children's families as well as reinforcing the day's teaching. Black and white copies of one side of the postcard can be found after each day's material. To order real postcards, turn to the inside front cover for details. Hand the postcards out and encourage children to find all their possessions before leaving the venue. Make sure that each child leaves with their authorised adult.

PART ② Setting up a holiday club

AIMS

When starting to think about running a holiday club, some big issues need to be tackled:

o What are the specific aims of running your holiday club?

o Is the holiday club part of the ongoing strategy of your church? If not, how does it fit in?

o Will the holiday club have the prayer support and financial support of your church?

o Do you have the people needed to make *Seaside Rock* a reality?

o Is there a wider vision for reaching the families of the children you are hoping will come to the club? If so, how can you make the most of the holiday club week?

o How will you follow up those children and families you have had contact with in the week? (See Part 8, page 78.)

Each holiday club will have its own specific aims. A programme such as *Seaside Rock* can provide a manageable, creative and fun way of reaching out to the children of your neighbourhood with the good news of Jesus. A holiday club can provide an excellent opportunity to blow any misconceptions away and to reveal to them a God who loves them passionately.

The broad aims of *Seaside Rock* are as follows:

o to introduce the children to Jesus through the stories and experiences of Peter

o to encourage the children to build their lives on Jesus the Rock

o to provide a fast-moving, fun and action-packed holiday club programme.

Alongside these broad aims, you may have some more specific aims. For example:

o to attract new children to join your Sunday groups or other children's activities

o to develop your leaders' gifts and experience

o to present the gospel to children who've never heard it

o to provide an opportunity for children to make an initial or further commitment to follow Jesus

o to get to know the children in your church

o to provide a project to encourage your church to work together

o to establish links with the children's families

o to encourage cooperation with other churches or groups in your area

o to launch an ongoing children's group based on the *Seaside Rock* theme

o to give parents a few mornings off in the school holidays.

Any or all of these aims may be appropriate, but you'll have to decide what you want *Seaside Rock* to achieve in your situation. If you have several aims, you'll need to decide which are the most important. You'll also need to evaluate *Seaside Rock* afterwards. Decide now how you'll do that. How will you measure success?

THE CHILDREN

Having set your aims, you'll be able to make other key decisions such as:

o Who will you invite to *Seaside Rock*?

o Do your aims relate to the children already involved in your church, or those outside it?

o How many children do you want to involve? If your main aim is to get to know the children better, you might need to restrict numbers. On the other hand, if you want to present the gospel to children who haven't heard it, you may want as many as possible to attend.

o What age range(s) do you want to target with *Seaside Rock*? Do you want to cater for an age range that is well represented in your groups, or one that isn't? Will you be able to tailor the activities in a way that will appeal to a wide age range? *Seaside Rock* is designed for use with children between the ages of five and eleven. You will find some thoughts about using the material with other age ranges in Part 8 on page 78.

DATES AND DURATION

Fix the date for your holiday club early enough for people to take it into account when they book their holidays. It is essential that dates do not clash with other holiday clubs in the area, activities already booked at your premises, holidays organised by local schools, holidays/camps for local Boys' Brigade, Girls' Brigade, Cub or Brownie groups, carnivals or other local events. The potential leaders' availability will have the most effect on the duration of your holiday club. If most leaders need to take time off work, it may not be practical to run a full five-day club.

Whatever your plans, it is good practice to inform OFSTED in writing of your *Seaside Rock* club. However, you must by law register *Seaside Rock* if you are meeting for more than two hours a day, for six days or more in the year. Remember that other follow-up events may take you over your total of six days. If your event does not exceed this limit, but you have under eights in your group, you must still inform OFSTED. If in doubt, phone OFSTED and check with the Local Day Care Advisor – he or she is there to help! Of course, there are many ways to use *Seaside Rock* – perhaps as an after-school club, Saturday club or a Sunday teaching programme. Part 8 gives some ideas for adapting *Seaside Rock*.

TEAM MEMBERS

CORE PLANNING TEAM

All the helpers should be involved in planning and preparing for *Seaside Rock*, but you will need a smaller team to coordinate things and make some initial decisions. As well as the holiday club's overall leader, this should include your most experienced leaders, your minister and your children's workers.

LEADERSHIP ROLES

There are many different roles for leaders in *Seaside Rock* (see Part 3). It's important to note that your leaders do not all have to be experienced children's workers. Many people in your church will be quite capable of leading a small group of children after some initial basic training; and others will be suitable for supporting roles, such as

musicians, registrars and providing refreshments. Of course, many of the leaders with these supporting roles may be group leaders as well. Here are the minimum recommended adult-to-child ratios.

ADULT-TO-CHILD RATIOS

The recommended adult-to-child ratios are as follows:

> **for 0–2 years**
> one adult to every three children (1:3)
>
> **for 2–3 years**
> one adult to every four children (1:4)
>
> **for 3–8 years**
> one adult to every eight children (1:8)
>
> **for over-eights**
> one adult for the first eight children, followed by one for every twelve (1:12).

There should always be more than one adult for any group and one should be female.

Seaside Rock is an ideal opportunity to develop and nurture the gifts and experience of the teenagers in your church, in a structured and supervised environment. Bear in mind, though, that for the purpose of child protection matters, a child is anyone under eighteen. In other words, if you have a number of teenage helpers, you will need more adult leaders, not less. At first sight this may seem odd, because teenage leaders can be extremely helpful and competent, and can therefore make the adult leaders' job much easier. But it makes sense if we understand that even the most competent helpers will need to be mentored and encouraged if their gifts are to be developed to their full potential. Avoid the temptation of only giving your younger helpers the mundane or less challenging tasks. If you are aiming to stretch your helpers, then they will need the help and support of an adult leader.

APPOINTING TEAM MEMBERS

Make all team members aware of the current legislation and how it affects this kind of activity. The welfare of the children you hope to reach through *Seaside Rock* is of paramount importance. We are concerned for their spiritual welfare, but also for their physical and emotional welfare. Sadly nowadays, children are at risk as much as ever before, and it is our duty to do all we can to ensure their safety and well-being as we aim to show them God's love. All churches should have clear child protection policies. If you have an established procedure for your church, all of the holiday club team must go through that process.

If you don't have a procedure in place, a special club

week may well be a good opportunity to establish one. The following notes outline the main issues.

UK LAW

(If using **Seaside Rock** outside the UK, check current legislation and what is required.)

The government has published a code of practice for groups working with children. It is called *Safe from Harm*, and it contains a number of guidelines for good practice. Most denominations now have established good practice policies based on *Safe from Harm*, and it is important that you work according to the one that applies to you. For further advice or information in the UK, contact the Churches' Child Protection Advisory Service (CCPAS) on 0845 120 4550.

Safe from Harm contains guidelines rather than law, but you need to show that you have taken them into consideration. In fact, if you ignore such good practice your insurance may be invalid.

One important action is to ensure all those with access to children under eighteen (volunteers or in paid employment) make a signed declaration of any criminal conviction, including those 'spent' under the Rehabilitation of Offenders Act 1974, along with details of cautions, reprimands or warnings. Your denomination may require you to make use of the Criminal Records Bureau, which started functioning in England and Wales in April 2002. CCPAS can advise you on this too.

Failure to take the necessary steps could lead to a claim of negligence against the church if a child comes to any harm at the hands of anyone working with them in a voluntary capacity. 'Harm' includes ill-treatment of any kind (including sexual abuse), or impairment of physical or mental health or development. You should ask all potential team members to sign a form such as the one below. Emphasise that it represents positive action for good practice, and does not imply any slur or suspicion. Obviously, the nature of the form is sensitive and should be handled with care. Ensure that confidentiality is maintained. In accordance with the Data Protection Act, do not divulge any information to third parties.

If anyone gives a 'yes' answer, allow the individual to explain this disclosure personally or by letter. If you are in any doubt about the person's suitability, consult your church leader. As well as the declaration form, it is recommended that potential team members offer one name as a referee. Questions to ask a referee might include:

o In what capacity have you known the applicant, and for how long?

o How willing and able is he/she to work with others?

o How suitable would you consider him/her for work with children and young people?

o Are there any relevant details about this applicant which cause you concern?

Do not allow people not known to you to have unsupervised access to children.

CONFIDENTIAL DECLARATION FOR POTENTIAL TEAM MEMBERS

Guidelines from the Home Office following the Children Act 1989 advise that all voluntary organisations, including churches, take steps to safeguard the children who are entrusted to their care. You are therefore asked to make the following declarations:

Do you have any current or spent criminal convictions, cautions, bindovers or cases pending? **Yes** ☐ **No** ☐

Have you ever been held liable by a court for a civil wrong, or had an order made against you by a matrimonial or a family court? **Yes** ☐ **No** ☐

Has your conduct ever caused, or been likely to cause, harm to a child or put a child at risk, or, to your knowledge, has it ever been alleged that your conduct has resulted in any of these things? **Yes** ☐ **No** ☐

Signed   Date

Because of the nature of the work for which you are applying, this post is exempt from the provision of Section 4(i) of the Rehabilitation of Offenders Act 1974, by virtue of the Rehabilitation of Offenders Act 1974 (Exemptions) Order 1975, and you are therefore not entitled to withhold information about convictions which, for other purposes, are 'spent' under the provisions of the Act. In the event of an appointment, any failure to disclose such convictions could result in the withdrawal of approval to work with children in the church.

TRAINING TEAM MEMBERS

Undertaking some basic skills and knowledge training is vital for the success of the holiday club. You should aim to have at least two sessions together in preparation, and you should ensure that these are more or less compulsory for team members. As part of these sessions, the vision and practicalities of *Seaside Rock* can also be outlined.

See Part 4 for outlines for two training/preparation sessions.

VENUE

Choosing a venue is a very important issue. Sometimes a community hall or school is a well-equipped, neutral venue that can be non-threatening for children and parents outside the church. However, you may wish to use this opportunity to introduce the children and parents to your church building. This can also help save on the cost of hiring an alternative venue. The venue does need to have enough space for the number of children and the type of activities you are planning. You will need access to the venue for several days before the holiday club to ensure the necessary preparations can be made.

LEGAL REQUIREMENTS

Even if you don't need to register your holiday club under the Children Act, carefully consider the following requirements laid down by the Act as sensible guidelines to be interpreted with common sense. If you must register, you won't have any choice!

Requirements for accommodation state that the premises should be warm, clean and adequately lit and ventilated, with clearly marked emergency exits. The minimum unencumbered floor space to be provided for children aged five to eight years is 25 square feet (2.3 square metres) per child. In other words, be careful about very large numbers of children in a small hall, and work out the maximum number of children who can attend.

The premises you use should meet Health and Safety requirements. Check that the owners of the premises have complied with all the requirements. Ideally there should be one toilet and one hand basin for every ten children. Disposable towels or hot-air hand driers are preferable to roller towels. If you are preparing food on site, you will need to be inspected by the Environmental Health Officer. The person with overall responsibility for the catering

arrangements should have the minimum of the Basic Food and Hygiene Certificate. Smoking should not be permitted on the premises. Children should not be allowed unsupervised access to the kitchen.

SETTING UP THE ROOM

The holiday club will be greatly enhanced if the main room you are using is transformed into a seaside paradise! This will help create a wonderful atmosphere and spark the children's imagination. A suggested venue layout is given opposite. You will need to think about how you can transform your venue into a seaside location. The creative use of cardboard, wood, paint and other materials can make a real difference. Think about what you can hang from the ceiling, cover the walls with and put on the floor.

To transform the area you could:

o   Cover the walls with sheets which have been painted to look like the sea, and with white fluffy clouds. The overhead projector screen could be a big rectangular-shaped cloud in the sky!

o   Make Peter's house out of cardboard boxes.

o   Serve refreshments from an 'ice cream stand'.

o   Decorate the hall with bunting, life-belts, coloured posters etc.

o   Have registration take place under a coloured umbrella, using canvas chairs or deckchairs.

o   Construct a sandpit.

THE STAGE AREA

You will need a focal point at the front from which the Lifeguard can run the programme. On the stage, create a seaside area, with Peter's house (which is built on rock) on one side, standing next to the sandy shore of the Sea of Galilee – you could use play sand for the beach. The Rock Band could be in or near Peter's house, and the majority of the action can then happen by the sea, which is where the OHP/projector screen should be located.

ROCK POOL LOCATIONS

The rest of the room can be split up into Rock Pools, in which the Rock Groups are located. Colour-coded signs could be created to highlight the location of the groups. It may be best to keep chairs out of the way, except for those who cannot sit on the floor, so that the room can be used for the energetic sections of the programme without objects getting in the way.

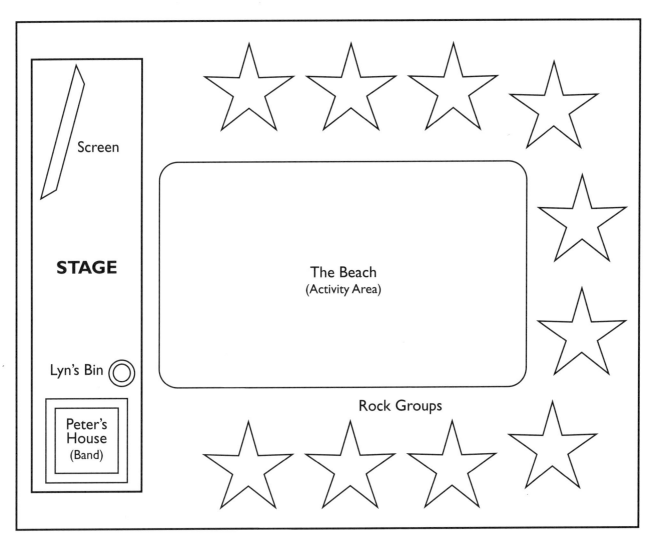

Screen

STAGE

Lyn's Bin

Peter's House (Band)

The Beach
(Activity Area)

Rock Groups

FINANCES

Work out a budget in advance. Work out what you'll need money for.

Examples might include:

o craft materials

o refreshments

o materials for the scenery

o photocopying/printing costs

o hire of premises

o hire of equipment such as video projector

o *Seaside Rock* books for your leaders

o resources such as the *Seaside Rock* video and *Seaside Rock* postcards.

o prizes or presents for the children (see the *Seaside Rock* website for details on awarding points throughout the week).

Do you need to do some fund-raising? Or will you charge a small fee for children to attend *Seaside Rock*?

PART ③ Areas of responsibility

A successful holiday club requires support teams to be set up and individuals to take responsibility for different areas of the programme. Listed below are some of the different teams you will need and some of the key roles people will need to assume before, during and after the event. Some people will be able to play more than one role for *Seaside Rock*.

DRAMA TEAM

A small team of five people should take responsibility for the *Seaside Rock* drama. These people need to be reasonably confident, able to project their voices and to act both big and silly! They should be willing to learn their lines and to practise each sketch until they can perform it with confidence.

Someone needs to take the responsibility of Props Manager, to collect and prepare all the props.

LIFEGUARD/PRESENTATION TEAM

The Lifeguard coordinates the upfront leading of the club. They will usually be the overall leader of the club, but this does not need to be the case. You will also need to find people to lead the following parts of the programme:

o Lyn the Bin (see page 41)

o Heather on the Weather (see page 41)

o Dancing on the Beach (see page 41)

The quality of presentation says a lot about the quality of your holiday club, so make sure your acetates are in focus, clearly written (ideally computer generated), in a legible font (such as Arial) and big enough for the children who are furthest away from the screen to see.

MUSICAL TEAM (THE ROCK BAND)

If you can't use live music, sing along to a CD player.

PRINTING AND PUBLICITY TEAM

A small team, including at least one computer literate person, should take responsibility for all the design, printing and publicity for *Seaside Rock*. Your aim should be to produce publicity that is visually impressive, consistent, accurate and attractive.

Publicity needs to be colourful, consistent, attractive and child-friendly. Use the *Seaside Rock* logo (either photocopied from this book or downloaded from the website).

The publicity team should take responsibility for:

o **posters and flyers** to advertise *Seaside Rock*.

o **a registration form** for the children to fill in (see sample version opposite).

o **a consent form** for parents/guardians/carers (see sample version opposite).

o **an invitation card or letter** to go with the appropriate forms.

o **helper's forms** for potential team members to indicate the roles they'd like to do – this should include the declaration form on page 13.

o **helper's notes and training materials** – even if someone else writes these, the printing and publicity team should be responsible for the layout.

o **name badges** for the team leaders and for any adults who are on site and part of *Seaside Rock*.

o **signs and notices** around the site, including the main hall, entrances, toilets and areas that are out of bounds. These should use the same typeface and colours as other materials to maintain the consistent *Seaside Rock* scheme.

o **prayer cards/bookmarks** – prayer pointers to help church members to pray for the holiday club before, during and after *Seaside Rock* events.

CPO produce a wide range of *Seaside Rock* publicity or other merchandise. For details, see the inside back cover.

SAMPLE REGISTRATION FORM

SEASIDE ROCK REGISTRATION FORM (please use a separate form for each child)

Seaside Rock will take place at *(venue)* from *(start date)* to *(end date)* *(give times)*
Please fill in this form to book a place for your child.

Child's full name	Sex: M/F
Date of birth	School

Please register my child for *Seaside Rock*.
Parent's/Guardian's signature

Parent's/Guardian's full name

Address

Phone number

I give permission for my details to be entered on the church database. ☐ Yes ☐ No

Nearer to the event, parents/guardians will need to fill in a consent form.

SAMPLE CONSENT FORM

SEASIDE ROCK CONSENT FORM (please use a separate form for each child)

Child's full name	Date of birth

Address

Emergency contact name	Phone number
GP's name	GP's Phone number

Any known allergies or conditions

I confirm that the above details are complete and correct to the best of my knowledge.

In the unlikely event of illness or accident I give permission for any necessary medical treatment to be given by the nominated first-aider. In an emergency and if I cannot be contacted, I am willing for my child to receive hospital treatment, including anaesthetic if necessary. I understand that every effort will be made to contact me as soon as possible.

Parent's/Guardian's signature   Date

REFRESHMENT TEAM

This team will play a vital role during the week. They will be responsible for:

o checking with the registration team about children with food allergies

o obtaining and preparing the refreshments for the children

o tidying up after the refreshments have been given out.

For this team to work efficiently choose one person to coordinate the group. Think about using disposable cups or bottles to save on washing-up time.

REGISTRATION TEAM

This team will be responsible for ensuring that the wording on the registration form is correct, welcoming everyone and registering the children when they arrive.

SECURITY PERSON

The person in charge of security will be responsible for ensuring that no child leaves the building unless they have permission to do so, and that only children or adults who are part of *Seaside Rock* are allowed to enter the building.

It is important for each adult to have an appropriate, clearly-labelled badge to identify them and their role. The children registered for *Seaside Rock* should have their own badge. Any adult or child on site not wearing an appropriate badge should be challenged.

If you are running a large holiday club, or if you are inviting a number of children who have no other contact with your church, it can be difficult to know whether the person collecting a child is the one who is authorised to do so. A form of 'receipt' slip is always useful, like the one below. The slip is given to the parent when they deliver their child and they have to show it when they come to collect the child.

SAMPLE COLLECTION SLIP

FRONT

Name

Group

BACK

Please make sure that you collect this slip when you bring your child each day. You will need to show it when you collect your child at the end of the morning. If your child is to be collected by someone else, please pass on this slip to that person.

If you will be unable to do this, or if your child is to go home on his/her own, please note this below, and return the slip to the registration desk immediately.

☐ Tick here if your child may go home on his/her own.

☐ Tick here if someone else is to collect your child. Write his/her name next to the day concerned.

Monday

Tuesday

Wednesday

Thursday

Friday

Thank you for your cooperation.

In the event of an emergency, the church telephone number is:

If, when dropping off the child, the parent signs the reverse to say that their child may go home alone or with someone else, the registrar should give that slip to the child's Rock Group leader during the session.

If a person wants to collect a child, but neither they nor the Rock Group leader has the slip, they should be referred to the overall leader, who will make sure that they are authorised to collect the child.

ROCK GROUP LEADERS AND ASSISTANTS

The Rock Group leader's role is to get to know the children so that they feel welcome and comfortable at *Seaside Rock*. The programme is designed to give the Rock Group leaders enough time in their Rock Pool areas to have meaningful discussions, including ones which apply the teaching programme to the children's lives.

Young or inexperienced team members can be assistant leaders. This helps the group leader, as well as allowing the assistants to develop their own gifts and skills under supervision.

If you have a large holiday club, you may choose to appoint Rock Group coordinators to oversee six or eight Rock Groups who are all in one age range. It is best if they do not have a group of their own.

Make sure your team members know that it is not appropriate for them to talk to a child alone in a room as this can be misinterpreted. The government has made it clear that such actions as guiding with a hand on the shoulder or comforting a distressed young child would not be considered inappropriate. It is a question of common sense in this area, but if in doubt, don't touch a child! You must have an agreed procedure in the case of a child disclosing abuse, or a situation which puts children at risk. Your church's Child Protection policy should outline a procedure. If not, contact CCPAS.

The Rock Group leaders have a specific responsibility for the children in their Rock Group during the week. They should sit with the children on all occasions, answering their questions and prompting them to discover more about Peter and about Jesus.

The Rock Group leaders should all be dressed in a suitable seaside manner. This could include T-shirts and caps (*Seaside Rock* ones are available), shorts and sandals.

FIRST-AIDER

Appoint at least one member of your team as the official first-aider. If possible appoint assistant first-aiders – a male for the boys and a female for the girls. These people will need a current first aid certificate, and access to a first-aid kit. You will also need an accident book to record any incidents or accidents. (This is essential in the event of any insurance claim. A record of the matter should be noted, along with details of action taken. It should be countersigned where appropriate.)

The entire team needs to know who the first-aiders are, any emergency procedures, including fire exits and assembly points, and where to access a telephone in case of emergency.

CRAFT AND EQUIPMENT

Someone should take responsibility for making sure that everything that is needed for the craft, beach games, creative prayer and Rock Group activities is in the right place at the right time.

TECHNICAL MANAGER

The amount of technology used will vary with the size and nature of each club. A technical manager could take responsibility for:

o   Balancing the levels on the public address system (this is especially important if you are running various musicians and presenters through the system).

o   Any TV, video, overhead projector or video projection equipment being used.

If you are running a club with less than fifty children, one or two TV sets can be used to show the video. To link two sets, you'll need a coaxial cable and a 'splitter', so that the video signal can be sent to both TVs. If you have more than fifty children, you should consider using a video projector. Either way, the sound would be better if played through your PA system rather than relying on the TV or projector speakers.

Find a suitable evening or weekend to put on these sessions for all team members. This training should be compulsory. Feel free to adapt them to your needs. These two session outlines should last two hours each.

SESSION 1:
THE BIG PICTURE AND LEADING A SMALL GROUP

Introduction: Basic outline of *Seaside Rock*

Section 1: Jesus' passion for children

Section 2: Leading a small group

Section 3: Keeping control of your group

Equipment: Flip chart and pens (or some other way of recording feedback and presenting material), slips of paper with Bible verses for section 1; slips with role play descriptions for section 2.

INTRODUCTION

Talk through the aims of this session together.

Do a basic introduction to *Seaside Rock* and the aims behind the holiday club. Discuss any issues that arise.

SECTION 1:
JESUS' PASSION FOR CHILDREN

Tell the group that you are going to look at exactly what Jesus said about children, and explore the way Jesus sees the children you are going to be serving. Give small groups a slip of paper each with the following Bible verses on:

o Matthew 18:1–5

o Matthew 18:6–9

o Matthew 18:10–14

o Matthew 19:13–15

o Matthew 21:12–17

Ask the groups to find and read the Bible verses together, discussing what the passage says about children. They should be prepared to feed back to the rest of the team. After a few minutes, ask the groups to talk about what they have learnt. The main points can be listed on the flip chart and are outlined below for your reference:

Matthew 18:3 Adults should become like children. Jesus explains in verse 4 that we should be like a humble child. A child's faith is deep and simple – our faith should be the same!

Matthew 18:5 Jesus identifies with children.

Matthew 18:6 We have a responsibility not to cause children to sin. Jesus reveals the depths of his love and his concern for children in their vulnerability.

Matthew 18:10 An order not to look down on children.

Matthew 18:10 Jesus recognises that there is a spiritual world beyond our own.

Matthew 18:14 Jesus' love is individual and universal for all, including children.

Matthew 19:14 All the blessings an adult can enjoy are also for children.

Matthew 21:16 Jesus here quotes Psalm 8:2.

Conclude this section by asking how a holiday club like *Seaside Rock* can help to bring children into a closer relationship with Jesus.

Thank God for his love of children and the privilege of sharing his love with the children of your area.

SECTION 2:
LEADING A SMALL GROUP

Leading a small group of children is a vital part of *Seaside Rock*. Group leaders will be the ones who get to know the children and build relationships with them. Sometimes these relationships can develop into long-term friendships. Understanding how these groups work and having guidelines is really important.

INTRODUCTION TO ROLE PLAY ACTIVITY

Ask the leaders to split into groups of approximately six or eight, in order to role play a small group of children at *Seaside Rock*. Some team members will be more comfortable with this activity than others, but encourage them all to participate! Tell the team that they are going to have a go at the Rock Pool Challenge for Day 2.

Firstly outline the activity to the team (on page 54), then give each member of the group one of the traits listed below on a slip of paper. One is the group leader, and the others represent different children's characters and behaviour. Tell the team not to show anyone their piece of paper, but to act it out during the activity as best they can. However, make sure the team doesn't overact and make their group leader's role a total nightmare! Each group will need a flip chart sheet and pens and should be given ten minutes for the task. When the role play is finished, give the groups a couple of minutes to share with each other their character descriptions.

Leader You are the leader of the group. Your group has lots of needs, and you should try very hard to include everyone in the discussion and keep the discussion on track.

Child 1 You are an intelligent child who knows all the answers and keeps putting their hand up to answer, or to ask a question. You don't call out or interrupt, though.

Child 2 You are a very shy, younger child, who is very slow in interacting with the group.

Child 3 You are a fidgeter who can't keep still, but you follow what is being discussed.

Child 4 You naturally interrupt all the time, but should respond to firm handling by your team leader. You should ask to go to the toilet at least once during the short group time.

Child 5 You listen well and follow all that your leader asks you do to, making a valuable contribution to the group.

Child 6 You are deeply committed to Jesus, and yet find it very difficult to articulate how you feel. You try very hard to contribute to the group.

Feedback from the role play

This activity is a good way of raising some of the issues involved in leading a small group. Have the flip chart ready to note down any interesting points that come up.

Talk first to the group leaders, encouraging them

that it will never be as difficult as this at *Seaside Rock*! Ask them to outline the characters in their group. Who was difficult to deal with? Who contributed? Who didn't contribute? Do they know why?

Discuss some of the issues raised by the characters; for example, how are you going to deal with children going to the toilet? By the time the feedback has finished, you should have a set of guidelines for leading a group. Below are a few 'dos' and 'don'ts' which may be worth adding to discussion at the end.

'DOS' AND 'DON'TS' OF LEADING A SMALL GROUP

Do learn the children's names quickly, and use them.

Do take notice of how each child behaves, reacts and interacts, so you can get to know each one.

Do take the initiative. Let them know clearly what you expect from the group, and how each member is valued and encouraged to participate.

Do be specific in your prompting and questions – this can help everyone contribute.

Do be aware that each child will come with their own needs.

Do be polite and patient, even if one or two children really annoy you!

Do add lots of enthusiasm to your group. The children will pick up on your attitude – you are a role model.

Do think creatively, for example how you sit, lie, kneel as a group to discuss things.

Do model what you expect the children to do, eg your response to what happens on the stage.

Do be careful to follow closely any instructions or notes you are given.

Do ask for help if you need it – you are not alone!

Do be careful with language – no jargon, complicated or inappropriate language.

Do pray for them and yourself as you lead the group.

Don't take favourites.

Don't be physical with them, as physical involvement can be misinterpreted.

NOTE: It is always better to have more 'dos' than 'don'ts'!

SECTION 3: KEEPING CONTROL OF YOUR GROUP

Give a few pointers on how to keep good control and maintain behaviour within groups. You could split the team into small groups to come up with their top tips, or simply talk through some of the issues.

You should encourage the team to be loving, firm and fair with the children. Establish any ground rules for the club and for the building and make sure that each Rock Group leader is aware of them, and able to support each other in the implementation of each rule. Make sure that these are recorded to ensure a safe, fun and successful week.

The key to establishing good discipline and control is relationship-building and clear expectations. This can be done by:

o Clearly stating and explaining expectations.

o Rewarding good behaviour.

o Praising them.

o Telling them when they haven't reached your expectations, and why.

o Explaining why clear boundaries are needed, and what would happen if everyone didn't follow the club rules.

o Recognising the positive actions of a child who usually misbehaves and encouraging them to behave better.

We need to understand that behaviour can sometimes be affected by:

o Physical factors, eg room, temperature

o Lack of preparation

o Poor resources

o Weather

o Poor presentation of the programme

o Disruptive influences

o What is going on at home

o Tiredness

o Personality clashes

o Previous events in the club

o Special needs, eg medical, behavioural, educational

o Lack of leadership/confidence of leader

o Inconsistency of rules between leaders

SESSION 2:
THE CHILDREN AND FINAL PREPARATIONS

Introduction and recap

Section 1: Working with children with special needs

Section 2: Working with children from other faith backgrounds

Section 3: Praying with children

Section 4: Practical preparations for the week

Prayer

EQUIPMENT

Flip chart and pens (or some other way of recording feedback and presenting material), OHP to show song lyrics and examples of the acetates to be used during the week.

Introduction

Outline the aims and content of your time together.

Recap on the training undertaken during the previous session, maybe going through the section on 'Keeping control of your group' if you didn't have time at the end of the last session.

SECTION 1: WORKING WITH CHILDREN WITH SPECIAL NEEDS

You need to look at the issue of working with children with special needs. Photocopy the following page and use as appropriate. Ask those with specific responsibility for children with special needs to outline their plans so that everyone is prepared. Without breaking confidentiality, discuss any children known to have a special need.

SECTION 2: WORKING WITH CHILDREN FROM OTHER FAITH BACKGROUNDS

This may not be obviously relevant for your club but make team members aware that we live in a multi-faith society. At school all children are made aware of this. It affects how they view the uniqueness of the Christian faith. Photocopy the following page and use as appropriate.

WORKING WITH CHILDREN WITH SPECIAL NEEDS

o Enjoy these children for their individuality, value and what they can offer. Some children with special needs may have distinctive areas of interest or talents that can be developed at appropriate times.

o Always find out as much as possible about the child before the start – their likes/dislikes, strengths/weaknesses, particular needs, and how best they can be included to make them feel safe and part of the group.

o Medical needs should be noted on the signed registration form. Pay special attention to the use of medication. Keep a record of medication given, noting time and quantity, initialled by two team members.

o Designate leaders to work one to one with children with challenging behaviour. Where appropriate, set up a buddy system so that they work closely with a peer. As far as possible, keep children with disabilities with their own peer group. Give all children opportunities to join in activities.

o Expect good behaviour from all children, but be tolerant of unusual behaviour, eg some children need to fiddle with something in their hands.

o Ensure all the children know what is planned for the day. Give children a five-minute warning when an activity is about to finish. Some children need to finish one activity before they can concentrate on another.

o Prepare each session with a range of abilities in mind. Think carefully about working with abstract ideas. These may be misunderstood and taken literally!

o Have a range of craft ideas. Check that you do not give a child with learning difficulties a task that is appropriate for their reading age but inappropriate for their actual age.

o If you have a child with hearing difficulties, make sure they sit near the front and that leaders have their face clearly on view (not lit from behind). If a loop system is available, check that it is working for this child. Discussion in small groups can be hard for deaf children. Try to reduce background noise.

o Do a risk assessment so that you are aware of any difficulties that may arise and take all possible action to avoid these.

WORKING WITH CHILDREN FROM OTHER FAITH BACKGROUNDS

Principles to work from:

o We will not criticise, ridicule or belittle other religions.

o We will not tell the children what their faith says or define it by what some of its adherents do.

o We will not ask children to say, sing or pray things that they do not believe or that compromise their own faith.

o We will respect the faith of the children.

o We will value and acknowledge the children's culture.

o We will use music, artwork and methods that are culturally appropriate.

o We will be open and honest in our presentation of the Christian faith.

o We will be open and honest about the content of our work with parents and other significant adults.

o We will seek to build long-term friendships that are genuine and not dependent upon conversion.

o Where children show a genuine interest in the Christian faith, we will encourage them, but be open and honest about the consequences. We will never encourage them to make decisions that could put them in danger.

There are some practical considerations. Many Asian communities (of all faiths, including Christian) are uncomfortable with bodily contact, especially between boys and girls. Does this mean you need to rethink your games? Moreover, many Asian girls may prefer to be in single-sex groups. Make allowances for this. Also be culturally sensitive about the food you offer – no pork products (including gelatine) for Muslims, while some Hindus don't eat eggs. Include a choice of snacks from various cultures. Acknowledge that children from other faith backgrounds have some understanding about the nature and person of God. Don't assume they know nothing and that what they know is wrong. Be open about what goes on in *Seaside Rock*. Never suggest that children keep things a secret. Remember that asking children to change faith may be dangerous or inappropriate – it could mean exclusion from the family or even death.

SECTION 3: PRAYING WITH CHILDREN

Talk through the notes below with the team, and make specific arrangements for your *Seaside Rock* week to allow children the space to pray.

When praying with children in a large group or all together, take care to use simple, clear, modern English. Keep your prayers brief, relevant and free from jargon. At the end of the session, thank God for the time you have had together, the friendships made and the things learnt. As the week progresses, you may want to pray all together about things that bother the children or that are in the news. Talking with God should be very natural and the children need to realise this. Explain that we say 'Amen' as a means of saying we agree. We don't have to close our eyes and put our hands together!

Some children may ask for prayer individually, or desire to respond to God by praying by themselves. Pray with a child in the main hall where you can be seen, ideally in a designated quiet area. If their request comes at an inconvenient time, make sure you find time to be with the child later, or pass them on to a leader who is free.

A child may want to make a commitment to Jesus, maybe for the first or tenth time! Ask the child if they have any questions, and talk about the important step they are about to make. Explain clearly and simply what it means to follow Jesus. Pray a simple prayer with them, pausing to allow them to repeat each phrase out loud. An example of such a prayer is below.

> Dear Heavenly Father,
>
> I'm sorry for all the things I have done wrong.
>
> Thank you that Jesus loved me so much that he came to earth and died on the cross for me, so that I can be forgiven. Please forgive me. Please help me to be more like Jesus each day and to be his true friend.
>
> **Amen.**

Assure the child that God hears us when we pray to him, and that he has promised to forgive us and help us be his friends if we really want to. You may wish to photocopy the prayer on to a piece of

card, with space for the child's name and the date. Encourage them to show it to their parent or carer when they get home, if that is appropriate. Make sure they know about all the other activities that the church runs for children in their age group. *Would you like to know Jesus?* and *Want to be in God's family?* (SU) both help explain what it means to follow Jesus. Details are on the inside front cover.

SECTION 4: PRACTICAL PREPARATIONS FOR THE WEEK

Talk though a typical day with the team, helping them understand each part of the programme and what is expected of them throughout the session.

If possible, give the actors who play Heather on the Weather and Lyn the Bin (and Peter, if you are not using the *Seaside Rock* video) an opportunity to introduce themselves. This will be fun, and will help the team to get a feel for both the teaching and the sillier elements of the programme. If you have the time and space, play one or two of the games. Learn the *Seaside Rock* song and watch an episode of the video.

Make sure that each team member is confident in their role, and is aware of everything they need to bring with them and all the practicalities.

Pray

It is a good idea to produce a small prayer card for the members of your church to inform their prayers. Hand these out and ask the team to pray in small groups for the whole club, the leaders, children and all the preparations. Pray big, bold prayers of faith for what Jesus is going to do at *Seaside Rock!*

HOLIDAY SNAPSHOTS – MEMORY VERSES

Traditionally, when Jewish children learnt the scriptures, they sang them! It remains one of the best ways for children to memorise the scriptures. *Seaside Rock* has a memory verse songs for each of the five day's memory verses. These songs can be learnt separately, but they can easily be put together in a medley format. A recording of them is on the *Seaside Rock* CD and on the *Seaside Rock* single.

Children learn better if they are active, rather than passive! Invent actions for the songs that are appropriate for your group (suggestions for the *Seaside Rock* theme song and memory verse songs are on pages 26 and 27).

Alternatively, introduce the memory verses using other ways. Here are a few ideas:

o   Write each word on a balloon. Gradually pop them as the children repeat the verse, until they can remember the verse unaided.

o   Put all the words on different pieces of card. Hang a washing line going across the room, with the cards pegged to it (maybe cut out in the shape of clothing). Gradually take the pieces of card down as the children learn the verse.

o   Photocopy the memory verse onto card, chop it up and give it to the groups as a jigsaw puzzle. The children can learn the verse in groups and tell the rest of the club what they have learnt.

o   Put the memory verse on an acetate in non-permanent pen. Read it through a few times, then rub out some of the words. Repeat until the whole memory verse has been rubbed off.

Each day's postcard contains the memory verse. This will mean the children can practise it at home.

Note: On each postcard is the full memory verse from the CEV Bible. The memory verse songs are a paraphrase.

MEMORY VERSE SONGS

Day 1

Simon answered,
'You are the Son of the living God!' Matthew 16:16
'You are the Son of the living God!' Matthew 16:16
Oooooohhhhhhhh! Yeah!

Simon answered,
'You are the Son of the living God!' Matthew 16:16

Day 2

Jesus said,
'If you listen and obey you're like a wise man,'
'If you listen and obey you're like a wise man,'
'If you listen and obey you're like a wise man who built his house on rock.' Matthew 7:24

Jesus' words I sing once more!
'If you listen and obey you're like a wise man who built his house on rock.'

Day 3

With only a word, Jesus healed the sick!
With only a word, Jesus healed the sick!
Verse 16, Matthew 8,

Isn't Jesus really great?
With only a word, Jesus healed the sick!

Day 4

If we confess our sins to God, he can be trusted – to take our sins away! (away, away)
If we confess our sins to God, he can be trusted – to take our sins away! (away, away)

1 John chapter 1, verse 9,
This is true every time!
If we confess our sins to God, he can be trusted – to take our sins away! (away, away)

Day 5

So, come to Jesus, the living stone!
So, come to Jesus, the living stone!
He's alive for evermore!

1 Peter 2, verse 4,
So, come to Jesus, the living stone!

*All songs written by Dave Godfrey © Daybreak Music 2002 (available on the **Seaside Rock** CD and the **Seaside Rock** single). The music for the memory verse songs is on the website www.scriptureunion.org.uk/seasiderock*

Day 1 Memory verse song actions:

Simon answered:
Pretend to pick up a telephone to answer it – use thumb and little finger to make the shape of a telephone.

You:
Point to another person.

are the Son:
Put one hand on the head of a pretend small child next to you.

living God:
Raise other hand in the sky.

Matthew 16:16:
On the 'six' show six fingers, on the 'teen' show ten!

Oooh! Yeah!:
Spin on the 'Oooh' and then jump on 'yeah!'

Instrumental bars:
Knobbly knees dance

Day 2 Memory verse song actions:

If you listen:
Put one hand behind ear and lean to the side as if trying to listen.

and obey:
Stand up with both thumbs up!

you're like a wise man:
Fold arms, lean back and nod.

who built his house on rock:
Put fists on top of each other.

Matthew 7:24:
Use seven, then two, then four fingers to show the reference.

Jesus' words I sing once more:
Move both hands, with thumbs up, to the beat – gradually raising them higher in the air.

Instrumental bars:
Build fist on fist.

Day 3 Memory verse song actions:

With only a word Jesus healed:
Pretend to be really ill.

the sick:
Hold hands out to show healing with a big smile on your face!

verse 16, Matthew 8:
For sixteen use same action as Day 1, then for eight show two lots of four fingers.

Isn't Jesus really great!
Make superhero poses.

Instrumental bars:
Fast Egyptian dancing.

Day 4 Memory verse song actions:

If we confess our sins to God:
Bow down on one knee in a humble way.

he can be trusted:
Cross arms in front of face, whilst rising to a standing position.

to take our sins away:
Cup hands together as though holding something on word 'take', then in a sweeping action throw it away, moving to the right each time. (On repeat go to left.)

1 John 1:9:
Show one finger of your right hand, then one finger of your left hand, then nine fingers to denote the reference.

This is true, every time:
Point to wrist/watch.

Instrumental bars:
Do the twist.

Day 5 Memory verse song actions:

So, come to Jesus:
Beckon with hand, then put arms outwards to form a cross shape on the two syllables of 'Jesus'

the living stone:
Do a fist on fist action on each syllable of 'liv-ing stone'.

he's alive for evermore:
Roll hands over and over each other.

1 Peter 2:4:
Hold up one, then two, then four fingers on one hand!

Instrumental bars:
Pretend to play a trumpet or trombone.

SEASIDE ROCK THEME SONG

Do the diggety dig in the rockety rock,
Spin yourselves around.
Build the brickety brick then go knockety knock,
And dance on solid ground,
At the Seaside Rock!

I'm at the beach here, with my friends,
Soaking up the sun,
Seaside Rock is really mint,
Come and join the fun! Oooh! Yeah!

Like Seaside Rock, from head to toe
You're full of flavour too.
Let his name run through your life,
Jesus Christ loves you! Oooh! Yeah!

Dave Godfrey © Daybreak Music 2002

SUGGESTED ACTIONS TO *SEASIDE ROCK*

Chorus

Line 1: Dig with pretend spade to the rhythm, followed by right fist on left fist twice and left fist on right fist twice.

Line 2: Spin yourself around, with hands palm outwards at chest height, moving to the beat.

Line 3: Build quickly with four bricks on the floor, then knock, with one hand on hip, on a pretend door.

Line 4: Dance, then 'John Travolta' style point with one hand on the word 'rock'.

Verse one:

Line 1: Put your arm around another child.

Line 2: Spread hands outwards, looking at the beautiful sky.

Line 3: 'John Travolta' style point with one hand on the word 'rock' followed by double thumbs up.

Line 4: Beckon to those around with both hands, crouch down and explode on 'yeah!' and bounce before going into the chorus.

Verse two:

Line 1: 'John Travolta' style point with one hand on the word 'rock', touch head and toes.

Line 2: Move hands up body with both body and hands shaking.

Line 3: Run to the rhythm.

Line 4: Hands outwards to form cross shape on 'Jesus' and 'Christ', then double point to someone on 'you', crouch down and explode on 'yeah!' and bounce before going into the chorus.

Fill (between first and second time through the song on the CD): You could try two bars of front crawl, backstroke, breaststroke and butterfly arm actions!

THE SEASIDE ROCK THEME SONG

THE GOLDEN PALACE DRAMA SCRIPTS

CAST

SIR ROBERT McDODGY: Rich building contractor who appears in episodes 1, 5 and B.

CHRIS: Younger brother (or sister) to Phil. He is an innocent, fun-loving, childlike character. Chris appears in all episodes.

PHIL: Older brother (or sister) to Chris, with a bit more experience and brain! Phil appears in all episodes.

POSTMAN PETE: Pete appears each time with bare feet and his postbag full of mail. He appears in episodes 1, 2, 3, 4 and 5.

GLADYS TEATIME: Well-dressed, overpowering building inspector who visits the site and carries a clipboard with her at all times. Gladys appears in episodes 3, 4 and 5.

Note: *All characters can be played by either male or female actors. Change the names to suit the gender of the actors.*

INTRODUCTION:

The *Golden Palace* is based on Jesus' story of the wise and foolish builders. Phil and Chris are two 'big kids' (brothers or sisters) who live near the Sea of Galilee in more modern times. Phil is the older of the two, and Chris is mad on building, particularly with Lego. Due to a misunderstanding on Day 1,

Phil and Chris are commissioned to build a palace for the king by the end of the week. They spend the next three days not getting very far. On the final day, using 'banana power', they manage to finish the construction. The only problem is, as Gladys Teatime (the building inspector) has already pointed out, they have built on sand. When Postman Pete pretends to be the king in his new palace, the whole thing (made out of cardboard boxes) collapses and they have to flee the wrath of the building contractor Sir Robert McDodgy. Phil and Chris eventually learn that if you are going to build anything, it needs to have good foundations.

The episodes should be played with lots of silliness, slapstick and speed. They are loosely connected to the theme for the day, but they don't try to make any serious teaching points. They are a fun few minutes to conclude the children's experience each day at *Seaside Rock*!

Sketches 1–5 stand alone, with one episode for each day of the holiday club. Episodes A and B have been written for the family services that might precede and follow *Seaside Rock*. They are not essential, but will help the wider church get a feel of what is going on.

You can find the drama scripts on the website – www.scriptureunion.org.uk/seasiderock

---

EPISODE A

SUMMARY: Episode A introduces us to Chris and Phil. They are in their house playing, and Phil is having fun picking on Chris…

PROPS: Lego *(hotel plus bricks)* in plastic box, ball, big jacket, scarf, boots, sunglasses, sandwich box, cuddly toy, stick of *Seaside Rock*, spade, foam, builder's hat.

TEACHING LINK: Introduces the characters and the building theme.

(Chris dashes in – nearly stumbling over as he reaches the front. He is preciously guarding a large box of Lego, with a nearly completed structure made out of the bricks in the colours of his favourite football team.)

CHRIS:
(To himself.) At last, some peace and quiet! *(To the congregation.)* Morning everyone! *(Awaits reply.)* I'm

Chris and I've managed to escape for a few moments from my big brother, Phil. I need to spend a bit more time finishing off my new, superduper, Colchester United *(insert appropriate team!)* Lego team hotel. *(He starts singing one of his favourite football songs.)*

PHIL:
(Enters, whistling the 'Match of the Day' theme tune and kicking a ball.) And Beckham wriggles his way into the penalty area… he shoots… GOAL! Hi there kid, what you up to?

CHRIS:
(Hiding the 'hotel' from Phil.) Go away. I'm busy finishing off something.

PHIL:
What sort of something? *(Bounces ball on Chris's head.)*

CHRIS:
Ow! The sort of something that big brothers don't need to know about!

PHIL:
Ooooh! You're a bit touchy this morning! You building Lego again? (*Bounce.*)

CHRIS:
Yeah. (*A bit disappointed that Phil has worked it out, and now very keen to show him what he is making.*) It's the Colchester United team hotel.

PHIL:
It's a bit small, isn't it? Mind you, you could probably fit all the players' talent in there! (*Laughs!*)

CHRIS:
Huh! (*Turns away and goes back to building.*)

PHIL:
Anyway, I've brought you a present. (*Phil moves to get present, Chris follows.*)

CHRIS:
Really? (*Excited, then cautious.*) If it's a tea-towel, it's your job to dry the pots.

PHIL:
No. It's just that I know how much you want to be a builder. I've been investigating how I could turn you into a proper builder!

CHRIS:
Ooh!

PHIL:
First of all you need a builder's jacket. (*Puts a large jacket on Chris.*) Then you need a big pair of boots. (*Puts big wellies or boots on, quickly.*) Then you need your scarf around your neck, sunglasses on your nose, sandwich box for your lunch, cuddly toy in case you get lonely, a stick of seaside rock to suck, spade for digging, your bricks for building, a lovely white beard (*Phil puts a shaving foam beard on Chris.*) and a builder's hat. (*Also filled with shaving foam.*)

CHRIS:
Are you sure I need the beard?

PHIL:
Yep!

CHRIS:
Do I look like a builder now?

PHIL:
Yep!

CHRIS:
I'd love to be a builder.

PHIL:
(*To the audience, as he is giving away a sneaky clue to the week's sketches.*) Well, maybe this could be your week!

CHRIS:
It's very difficult to move in this lot.

PHIL:
In that case you won't be able to catch me when I nick your team hotel…
(*Dashes off stage. Chris struggles to catch up, dropping bits of clothing as he leaves.*)

PHIL:
I'm off to the seaside – see you later!

CHRIS:
(*Shouting.*) Wait… I want my hotel back!

EPISODE I

SUMMARY: The first full episode introduces the main characters and is a series of discoveries. Sir Robert McDodgy discovers that it is the king's birthday next week and decides to build a palace for the king's birthday present. He (literally) bumps into Chris and Phil who are fighting over the Lego hotel that Chris has made, which Phil has hidden. McDodgy thinks the hotel is a real one and invites Chris and Phil to build for him. Chris and Phil agree, and then realise what they have let themselves in for. They panic, before Phil remembers something he's read and they decide to take up the challenge!

PROPS: Letter, contract, pen, Lego hotel, cardboard boxes on stage, two spades (hidden somewhere on stage), chase sequence music.

TEACHING LINK: Just as Jesus chose Peter, Phil and Chris are chosen unexpectedly for an important job.

PETE:
(*Enters singing.*)
Postman Pete, Postman Pete, Postman Pete with the stinky feet.
Early in the morning, just as day is dawning.
You can smell him coming down your street!

Morning kids! My name's Pete, and I'm the postman on this street! Did you like my new song? Tell you what, every time you see me on the street why not sing the little song with me? (*Teach the children the words again, then go off and start the sketch again.*)

PETE:
(*Enters singing.*) Very good! I'm trying to find Sir Robert McDodgy, the very rich building contractor. Now where is he? He's impossible to find!
(*McDodgy enters singing 'Oh I do like to be beside the seaside'.*) There you are, McDodgy.

MCDODGY:
Morning, Pete! How are your feet?

PETE:
Bit smelly as usual! Here's your mail. See ya! (*Pete walks off.*)

MCDODGY:
(*Looks at the letter with real excitement.*) Hooray, I love getting mail. (*Reading.*) 'Dear Sir Robert McDodgy, Top Building Contractor.' (*To the children.*) That's me! (*Opens the letter and reads.*) 'This is a quick note to let you know that his majesty, the king, will be celebrating his birthday here next week. Yours, Mad Magnus, the Mayor.' Wow! The king is coming here. This could be my moment! Think, think, what birthday present could I give the king? Hmmmm. I know! I could build him a… (*Phil enters in a rush and carefully places the hotel somewhere at the front. Chris enters in a rush!*)

CHRIS:
Come back here, you sneaky thief!
(*Phil begins to run again. Chris and Phil then chase each other to appropriate background music, before Phil accidentally bumps into Sir Robert McDodgy.*)

MCDODGY:
Ow!

PHIL:
Ow!

CHRIS:
Ooops!
(*Slight pause, before Phil dives around the other side of McDodgy for cover. McDodgy is then caught in the middle of the Phil and Chris.*)

CHRIS:
Give me my hotel back!

PHIL:
You can't have your hotel back.

CHRIS:
But I built it, it's *mine*… I need it…

PHIL:
You can't have it.

CHRIS:
I'll tell Mum!

MCDODGY:
Excuse me, did you say you'd built a hotel?

CHRIS:
Yeah, and he won't give it back.

MCDODGY:
Well, listen up my friend. I need someone who can build me a hotel. (*Chris and Phil freeze. McDodgy begins to prance around in front of Phil and Chris in a flamboyant style.*) A big hotel. A massive hotel. In fact, I need someone to build me a palace… this week! Could you do that?

CHRIS:
What?

MCDODGY:
I'd like *you* to build me one of your hotels, except bigger. I need a palace as a special birthday present for the king! I want you to build it with strong foundations – it needs to be built to last.

PHIL:
How much?

MCDODGY:
Pardon?

PHIL:
How much will you pay us?

MCDODGY:
Are you a builder too?

PHIL:
Well, sort of!

MCDODGY:
(*Puts his arms around the shoulders of Phil and Chris.*) I'll pay you £500 each if you can build me a palace within a week.

CHRIS:
Wow!

PHIL:
Awesome!

MCDODGY:
Can you start today?

PHIL:
Yeah.

MCDODGY:
Great, sign here. (*McDodgy pulls out a contract which Phil and Chris sign. He then leaves contract, with Phil and Chris.*) Oh, make sure you keep an eye out for Gladys Teatime, the building inspector – she has the power to stop you building! I'll be in touch. (*Exits stage in a happy mood.*)

PHIL:
£500! Awesome!

CHRIS:
Mega!

PHIL:
Tell you what, if I'm gonna get £500 at the end of the week, I won't need your little hotel. I hid it under the cardboard box over there.

CHRIS:
Thanks. (*Goes over and rescues his Lego hotel.*) Hey, £500 isn't bad for building a Lego palace, is it?

PHIL:
I've never been paid for building anything out of Lego in my life!

CHRIS:
Being paid so much is a bit strange though.

PHIL:
Yeah, it is a bit.
(*Pause, with Phil and Chris suddenly looking at each other in shock.*)

CHRIS:
You don't suppose he wants us to build a real palace, do you?

PHIL:
I don't know. I'll check the contract! (*Reads it out.*) 'I guarantee that by Friday we will have built a brand new palace for the King with seven bedrooms using… real bricks and real glass!'

PHIL AND CHRIS:
Arrgghh!

CHRIS:
We've never built a real house before!

PHIL:
I know!

(*Phil and Chris collapse into each other's arms in a panic.*)

PHIL:
Hold on. That book I was reading the other day showed me how to build a real house. (*Phil mimes out the next bit at some speed.*) It said, 'Dig a hole in the ground, put in the foundations.' That's the solid rocky bit underneath. 'Then put the bricks on top, add a bit of glass, find a roof and Bob's your uncle.'

CHRIS:
I haven't got an uncle called Bob – the only uncle I've got is called Tom!

PHIL:
No stupid – I mean, that's all there is to building a palace!

CHRIS:
And you think we can do all that?

PHIL:
Easy!

CHRIS:
Golden Palace – can we build it? (*said in Bob the Builder style!*)

PHIL:
Golden Palace – yes we can! (*Have team leaders primed to join in with 'Yes we can' response!*)

CHRIS:
Hey, that's cool! Let's try it again! (*Repeat both Phil and Chris' part for the children to join in.*) Golden Palace – can we build it?

PHIL:
Golden Palace – yes we can!

CHRIS:
Cool!

PHIL:
Come on then, here are Dad's spades. (*Finds two spades on the stage area, hidden somewhere.*) I know just the place to build a fantastic palace. (*Exits.*)

CHRIS:
(*Turning to the children.*) I have a funny feeling about this!

(*Chris and Phil exit off to the side of the stage area with spades over their necks, whistling 'Heigh-ho' from Snow White as they leave. Again, have leaders primed to join in the song as Phil and Chris leave.*)

EPISODE 2

SUMMARY: Phil and Chris begin the task of building the palace for the king. They tackle the difficult decision of where to build the palace – on sand (which is easier) or on rock (which is harder). By the end of the sketch they have managed to get nowhere and decide to sleep on this most important decision!

PROPS: Contract, spades, mobile phone, water pistol, some sand and rock which could be picked up at appropriate points in the sketch.

TEACHING LINK: Today's theme is Jesus' teaching about the wise and foolish builders, and so the sketch will bring out the key decision which is made in the parable.

(*Phil and Chris enter with spades over their heads whistling 'Heigh-ho'. Get everyone to join in, clapping along to the tune.*)

CHRIS:
Golden Palace – can we build it? (*Encouraging participation!*)

PHIL:
Golden Palace – yes we can!

CHRIS:
Hi kids. Do you realise we've been walking around with spades over our heads whistling for the last twenty-four hours?

PHIL:
Don't be stupid!

CHRIS:
When are we going to stop pretending to be dwarfs then?

PHIL:
Now! (*Brief pause.*) 'Cos we're here. This is the place where we're going to build the palace for that McDodgy chap.

CHRIS:
Oh yeah, that's why we've got the spades. Hey, we get £500 each if we manage to build the palace by the end of the week!

PHIL:
Just think, we'll be able to buy loads of sweeties.

CHRIS:
I could munch a wine gum.

PHIL:
I could chew a jelly tot.

CHRIS:
I could eat Auntie Alison…

PHIL:
You can't eat Auntie Alison!

CHRIS:
I can – Mum keeps saying she's a real sweetie! (*Breaks out in hysterical laughter, repeating the joke!*)

PHIL:
That's terrible! Anyway, the first thing we need to decide is where to build the palace. McPodgy said it had to have strong foundations.

CHRIS:
I thought you said we were going to build it here?

PHIL:
Yeah, that's right, but do we build it over here (*Standing in front of Peter's house.*) or do we build it over here (*Going nearer the beach.*)?

CHRIS:
Well, I can't see much difference between 'here' and 'here'. They sound the same to me!

PHIL:
They might sound the same, but they are very different.

CHRIS:
Let me guess… one gets more sun and one gets more rain? (*He brings out a water pistol and squirts everything.*)

PHIL:
No, you stupid sausage! The difference is that 'here' is more rocky, while 'here' is more sandy.

CHRIS:
I once knew a girl called Sandy. (*Gets hit on the head by Phil.*)

PHIL:
Concentrate! We need to build the palace either on sand or on rock.

CHRIS:
Well, *I* don't know where to build it! What do you think children – should we build on sand or on rock? (*Get the children to say where they think the building should take place!*)

PHIL:
Hold on, what's that smell?

PETE:
'Postman Pete, Postman Pete,
Postman Pete with the stinky feet.
Early in the morning, just as day is dawning.
You can smell him coming down your street!'
(*Encourage the leaders and children to join in.*)

CHRIS:
Hey Pete, we need your help!

PETE:
Postman Pete at your service. What's the problem?

CHRIS:
We don't know whether to build here on sand, or here on rock!

POSTMAN:
(*In a whimsical way.*) Well, I love to have gentle grains of sand running between my toes, and standing on rock is really uncomfortable! I'd go for sand! Got to go and deliver the rest of my letters – see you! (*He exits.*)

PHIL:
Hmmm. Building it on sand will be easier, because sand is easy to move and building it on rock will be harder, because rock is harder to move.

CHRIS:
What does the contract say?

PHIL:
(*Phil quickly checks the contract.*) It only says the palace should last a long time and have strong foundations!

CHRIS:
Why don't you ring up McBodgy, or whatever his name is, and ask him?

PHIL:
OK, good idea! (*Rings number on mobile.*) Excuse me Mr McStodgy, I mean McDodgy, it's Phil here. We were just thinking about exactly where you want us to build this palace. (*Takes phone away from ear as if McDodgy is shouting at him.*) Oh, he's gone!

CHRIS:
What did he say?

PHIL:
He said, 'Just get on with it quick.'

CHRIS:
Well, digging sand is quicker than digging rock… he must have meant sand!

PHIL:
I suppose so! Hey, look at the time. It's getting really late. Maybe we should sleep on it.

CHRIS:
OK!
(*Lies down on the sand and pretends to sleep.*)

PHIL:
No, I didn't mean sleep on the sand, I mean we can think about it while we're asleep – then we can make a final decision in the morning. Come on…

CHRIS:
Hey kids. Golden Palace – can we build it?

PHIL:
Golden Palace – yes we can! (*Said with the children!*)

CHRIS:
Don't panic – we'll be back in the morning! (*To children, with worried look.*) I'm sure McPorky will be pleased with the progress so far! (*They exit whistling 'Heigh-ho' with their spades over their shoulders.*)

EPISODE 3

SUMMARY: Phil and Chris spend another day busy doing nothing! Phil has had a dream about their project in the night, which he interprets as confirmation that they should be building on sand. The boys then begin digging out the foundations with brief interruptions from Gladys Teatime, some seaweed and Postman Pete! After receiving an encouraging message from the building contractor, they decide to get an early night.

PROPS: Spades, handkerchief or tissue, waterpistol, seeweed (or green strips of paper), envelope cut into an 'E' shape.

TEACHING LINK: Peter discovered lots of wonderful things about Jesus. He would have had warm memories of the time Jesus healed his mother-in-law.

(Phil and Chris arrive carrying their spades and whistling 'Heigh-Ho'. Phil needs to be carrying his waterpistol in his pocket.)

CHRIS:
Golden Palace – can we build it? (*Encouraging participation.*)

PHIL:
Golden Palace – yes we can!

CHRIS:
Morning kids, morning Phil!

PHIL:
Good morning everyone. Did you sleep well, Chris?

CHRIS:
(*Struggling to blow his nose.*) Not really – I've got this really big bogey stuck up my nose!

PHIL:
I once wrote a poem about bogeys, do you want to hear it?

CHRIS:
Go on then…

PHIL:
(*Phil should act this out as he tells the rhyme.*)
I've got loads of habits
Like nibbling my toes;
Like collecting all my ear wax
For wiping on my clothes.

I've got loads of habits
Like when I eat my food,
I munch and slurp and gulp and burp,
But Mummy says I'm rude.

I pick my nose when playing,
I pick it during lunch;
And when I've gathered just enough
I have a bogey munch!

CHRIS:
You're a disgusting poet! Aren't we supposed to be digging?

PHIL:
Guess what?

CHRIS:
What?

PHIL:
As I was lying down in bed last night… (*Chris lies down.*)

CHRIS:
Like this?

PHIL:
Yep. And I was sound asleep.

CHRIS:
Like this? (*Massive snoring.*)

PHIL:
Yep. I had this dream. In my dream I got up and walked down here to the beach. (*Chris starts to sleepwalk.*) I walked over to the sandy bit and it was beautiful sunshine. (*Leans back as if soaking up the sun.*) Then I went over to the place where the rock is, and it rained! (*Squirts Chris with his hidden waterpistol.*)

CHRIS:
Hey, hold on…

PHIL:
Well, you got me yesterday! Anyway, if my dream is correct, we should be building this palace in the sand!

CHRIS:
Why?

PHIL:
Because I got wet on the rock.

CHRIS:
Are you sure?

PHIL:
Yes.

CHRIS:
OK!

(*Both start digging ferociously. Try to get a pattern going, taking it in turns to dig, and both stopping and mopping brows after every fourth dig. Meanwhile, Gladys Teatime enters looking really mean!*)

CHRIS:
Stop!

PHIL:
What?

CHRIS:
Stop digging! There's someone behind you!

PHIL:
What?

CHRIS:
There's someone behind you!

PHIL:
(*Phil turns around in panto style with Gladys hiding behind him as he turns.*) Oh no there isn't!

CHRIS:
(*Encouraging the children to join in.*) Oh yes there is!

PHIL:
Oh no there isn't!

CHRIS:
Oh yes there is!

PHIL:
Isn't!

CHRIS:
Is!

PHIL:
Isn't!

CHRIS:
Is! (*Eventually Phil does a sudden turn and is scared by Gladys.*)

GLADYS:
Excuse me, have you seen a new palace for the king anywhere around here?

CHRIS AND PHIL:
No.

GLADYS:
Sorry to bother you – goodbye!

CHRIS:
Told you!

PHIL:
Let's get digging! (*Resume digging.*)

CHRIS:
She was scary!

PHIL:
Stop!

CHRIS:
What?

PHIL:
Stop digging! There's something in the sand. (*Picks up some seaweed.*) Oh look, some seaweed. It reminds me of you!

CHRIS:
Why?

PHIL:
Because you've got a big bogey stuck up your nose!

CHRIS:
Ugh! Come on, keep digging! (*They start to dig again.*)

PHIL:
There's something very smelly down here!

PETE:
'Postman Pete, Postman Pete,
Postman Pete with the stinky feet.
Early in the morning, just as day is dawning.
You can smell him coming down your street!'
E-mail for you, lads! (*Postman Pete hands Phil a big envelope cut into an E shape.*)

CHRIS:
I've never had an e-mail that looks like that before. Who's it from?

PHIL:
It's from McDodgy. He says, 'I'm very much looking forward to seeing the new palace. You must be very tired from all your hard work. Why don't you take an early night and start again in the morning!'

CHRIS:
What a decent chap!

PHIL:
Yep, I've had enough for today. It's time for an early night. (*Picks up spade.*) Come on, we'll have to finish the palace in the morning.

CHRIS:
Hey kids! Golden Palace – can we build it?

PHIL:
Golden Palace – yes we can!

CHRIS:
See you tomorrow!
(*Phil and Chris exit whistling 'Heigh-ho'.*)

EPISODE 4

SUMMARY: Phil and Chris make a pact of friendship and brotherly love. However, when Chris goes back home to rescue his spade, the building inspector arrives. She is not impressed with their progress, and Phil puts all the blame onto Chris. When Chris discovers that he has been betrayed, he is deeply hurt. Phil is extremely sorry for lying and the pain he has caused Chris. He apologises and Chris forgives him. They misinterpret a postcard from McDodgy, and decide to take another early night.

PROPS: Spades, chair, tube of Smarties, postcard, lunchbox, chocolate biscuit, piece of cake, shaving foam, plate, chase sequence music.

TEACHING LINK: The promise of friendship, betrayal and forgiveness Phil finds in this sketch, mirrors Peter's promise of love, his betrayal and the forgiveness he finds from Jesus.

(*Phil and Chris arrive whistling 'Heigh-ho'. Only Phil has his spade with him. Chris is carrying a lunchbox containing a biscuit, cake, shaving foam and plate.*)

CHRIS:
Golden Palace – can we build it?

PHIL:
Golden Palace – yes we can!

CHRIS:
Morning everyone, morning Phil!

PHIL:
Back again.

CHRIS:
Another hard day's work ahead…

PHIL:
You know what? I was thinking last night how wonderful it is to have such a good friend as you. You're the best brother anyone can have!

CHRIS:
Thank you. It's funny you should say that, 'cos last night as I was cutting my toe nails, I suddenly thought 'Where would I be without Phil?' You're a great brother too.

PHIL:
We'll always be buddies, right?

CHRIS:
We'll always love and care for each other, right? (*They give each other a big hug!*)

CHRIS:
To celebrate this moment of friendship, I would like to share some things with you!

PHIL:
Great!

CHRIS:
(*Grabs a chair.*) Tell you what, you just sit here on this chair and shut your eyes while I'll give you three little presents!

PHIL:
Great!

CHRIS:
First one – open wide. (*Puts biscuit in Phil's mouth.*)

PHIL:
A chocolate biscuit – great!

CHRIS:
Do you like it?

PHIL:
Yep!

CHRIS:
Second one – open wide. (*Puts cake in Phil's mouth.*)

PHIL:
Cake – great!

CHRIS:
Do you like it?

PHIL:
Yep!

CHRIS:
Do you want the last present then?

PHIL:
Definitely!

CHRIS:
Alright! (*Sprays a lovely foam pie on the plate ready for Phil.*) Are you sure you want it?

PHIL:
Yep!

CHRIS:
Shall I let him have it? (*Wait for response from the children!*) You ready for this one, Phil?

PHIL:
Yep!
(*Chris puts the pie in Phil's face, with Phil making sure he keeps his mouth shut.*)

PHIL:
Yeuch!
(*Phil starts chasing Chris around the room, with appropriate music in the background. Eventually they collapse exhausted but laughing.*)

PHIL:
Very funny, little brother. Come on. We need to get digging!

CHRIS:
Oops, I've forgotten my spade. I'll just pop back and get it. (*Leaves the stage; Phil hums while he digs.*)

GLADYS:
(*Enters almost unnoticed.*) Excuse me?

PHIL:
(*Said without looking, not realising who he is talking to.*) Hello gorgeous!

GLADYS:
(*Acting very snooty.*) Is this the construction site for the new McDodgy palace?

PHIL:
Yep, and who might you be?

GLADYS:
My name is Gladys Teatime, building inspector for the County Council.

PHIL:
(*Suddenly paying attention and on his best behaviour.*) Oh, hello madam. How can I help?

GLADYS:
I've come to inspect your work so far. (*Looks around.*) Actually there's not an awful lot to inspect, is there?

PHIL:
Well, no, we've had a few problems. (*Making up excuses on the spot.*) It's my brother's fault really – he's terribly slow and he's made at least three big mistakes so far, which has cost us a lot of time.

GLADYS:
And why are you building on sand, when you could be building over here on the rock?

PHIL:
Well, that's Chris' fault too. He made us build here, because it's easier you see!

GLADYS:
I'm not very happy about this. I should force you to stop working.

PHIL:
Please don't. We've only just started! Come back tomorrow and it'll be very different then.

GLADYS:
OK, you've got until tomorrow. Goodbye. (*Chris bursts in, a bit out of breath, with his spade.*) Oh look, it's your incompetent brother. (*Exits.*)

CHRIS:
(*Freezes for a moment, then heads for Phil.*) Who was that and what does 'incompetent' mean?

PHIL:
That was the building inspector and 'incompetent' means 'totally useless'.

CHRIS:
What did you tell her?

PHIL:
Only that the reason we haven't got anywhere is your fault, and that the reason we were building on the sand was because you're… totally useless. (*Phil freezes, realising what he's done, and Chris bursts into tears.*)

CHRIS:
You horrible person. It's not all my fault!

PHIL:
No, I know. I'm really sorry.

CHRIS:
(*Wails uncontrollably.*) Ohhhhhh!

PHIL:
Chris, I'm really, really sorry.

CHRIS:
(*Through tears.*) How sorry?

PHIL:
(*Getting down on one knee.*) Really, really, really, really, really, really, really, really sorry.

CHRIS:
How sorry is that?

PHIL:
Really, really, really, really, really, really, really, really, really, really, I'll-give-you-my-only-tube-of-Smarties sorry.

CHRIS:
Really?

PHIL:
Yep. I shouldn't have said those things. Here are the Smarties. (*Brings them out of his pocket. They give each other a big hug.*)

CHRIS:
Thank you. I suppose we'd better get digging then.

PHIL:
At super speed! (*They start digging at a ridiculously silly speed, interrupted almost immediately by Postman Pete.*)

CHRIS:
Hold on, there's something smelly around here!

PETE:
'Postman Pete, Postman Pete,
Postman Pete with the stinky feet.
Early in the morning, just as day is dawning.
You can smell him coming down your street!'

CHRIS:
Morning Pete!

PETE:
Hi guys, here's your mail. (*Gives postcard to Phil and exits.*)

CHRIS:
Who's it from?

PHIL:
It's from McFroggy.

CHRIS:
What does he say?

PHIL:
He says, 'Hi there boys, I hope you're having a good day. I'm very much looking forward to seeing the palace in three days time. Don't work too hard. Yours, Robert McDodgy.'

CHRIS:
Have we got three more days to build then?

PHIL:
Yeah, I thought he'd be back tomorrow.

CHRIS:
We could go home early then.

PHIL:
Good idea.

CHRIS:
(*Spends a moment looking over the site.*) I think we've made some good progress! (*To everyone.*) Golden Palace – can we build it?

PHIL:
Golden Palace – yes we can!
(*They pick up spades and leave whistling 'Heigh-ho'.*)

EPISODE 5

SUMMARY: Phil brings along two bananas to give them the energy to build. Before they get a chance, McDodgy arrives and finds the palace hasn't been started yet. He disappears in search of the brothers, who with the help of their bananas (and a few children), manage to build the palace in no time at all! Gladys Teatime arrives, closely followed by Postman Pete and McDodgy. McDodgy pays Phil and Chris for their work before asking Pete to pretend to be the King in his new palace. Disaster strikes when Pete sits down and the house collapses around his feet. This leads to a lot of chasing about and to a lecture from Gladys Teatime about where they should have built. The sketch ends with an exasperated McDodgy chasing the two brothers off the stage.

PROPS: Spades, two bananas, two envelopes with 'money' in, loads of cardboard boxes, 'crash' sound effect, two children to help with the building.

TEACHING LINK: This sketch concludes the parable of the wise and foolish builders.

(Phil and Chris arrive whistling 'Heigh-ho'. Chris is carrying both spades, and Phil is carrying two bananas.)

CHRIS:
Golden Palace – can we build it?

PHIL:
Golden Palace – yes we can!

CHRIS:
Morning everyone, morning Phil! Hold on, how come I'm carrying both spades?

PHIL:
Because I'm carrying both bananas!

CHRIS:
Bananas?

PHIL:
Yep. These bananas are going to help us build!

CHRIS:
Can they dig, then?

PHIL:
No, stupid! Of course they can't dig! We're going to eat them and they are going to help us build this palace at superspeed. These bananas are full of *(Said in American accent.)* 'banana power'!

CHRIS:
Oh…

PHIL:
Where were we? I think we've dug deep enough – we need to start putting in the foundations… *(As Phil continues to talk, McDodgy begins to approach,*

singing from offstage. When Chris and Phil realise it is McDodgy they hide at the back of the stage.)*

MCDODGY:
(Singing.) 'Oh, I do like to be beside the Seaside Rock; Oh, I do like to be beside the sea; Oh, I do like to see the new golden palace…' Hold on, there's nothing here apart from a hole! Where are those two incompetent builders? *(Storms off in search of Phil and Chris.)*

PHIL:
Phew, that was close!

CHRIS:
I thought you said he was coming back in three days?

PHIL:
I thought he was… *(Pause.)* Oh! *(Realising.)*

CHRIS:
Oh?

PHIL:
Yeah!

CHRIS:
What?

PHIL:
Well, when you think about it, he probably wrote the postcard on Tuesday. We got it yesterday, two days after it was sent! That means *three* days after it was sent is today!

CHRIS:
Oh no! We haven't got a building yet!

PHIL:
No, but we do have two bananas. Here, take one of these and eat it.

CHRIS:
Bet I can eat my banana quicker than you!
(They eat their bananas very quickly, and go into hyper-drive and begin constructing the building out of loads of cardboard boxes stacked up at the back of the stage. They start talking in American superhero accents.)

PHIL:
(Choosing two children to help him.) Quick, you two – come and give us Banana heroes a hand.

CHRIS:
Wow, what a wonderful sight – banana power in action! *(A few moments later the building, or what there is of it, is complete. Just then, Gladys Teatime arrives.)*

GLADYS:
Ah, good afternoon gentlemen. I see you have a building for me to inspect today. How did you manage to build it so quickly?

CHRIS:
(Shouts out in excitement.) Bananas!

GLADYS:
(Turns towards Chris, shocked.) You rude person! *(McDodgy comes in, angry.)*

MCDODGY:
There you are. What's your mother doing here?

GLADYS:
Mother?

MCDODGY:
Grandmother, then!

GLADYS:
Why, you extremely rude… and smelly person… ooh, what a stink! (*She faints.*)

PETE:
'Postman Pete, Postman Pete,
Postman Pete with the stinky feet.
Early in the morning, just as day is dawning.
You can smell him coming down your street!'
Morning everyone!

MCDODGY:
(*Ignoring Pete and suddenly seeing the new palace.*)
Hold on – look at that! It's my Golden Palace… Oh you clever boys! (*McDodgy goes over and hugs Chris and Phil.*) I think its party time! Here you go, lads – £500 each as I promised! (*Hands over the envelopes to the boys.*)

CHRIS AND PHIL:
Wow, thank you! (*Chris and Phil move into the background.*)

MCDODGY:
Tell you what, Pete – give me your postbag. (*Pete gives McDodgy his postbag.*) Go into the palace and pretend to be the king – show us all how much you love your new palace!

PETE:
OK! (*He climbs into the palace and starts pretending to be the king*) Oh what lovely walls – what a fantastic view. Let me sit down on my royal throne for a moment. (*Pete tries to sits down on the cardboard boxes and ends up sending the boxes flying. Crash sound effect.*)

MCDODGY:
Oh no – my new palace is destroyed! (*McDodgy suddenly turns on Chris and Phil.*) You two! (*Chris and Phil start to run.*) Come back here! (*McDodgy, still holding Pete's bag, begins to chase Chris and Phil around the room.*)

PETE:
Come back with my mail! (*Pete starts chasing

McDodgy, who is chasing Chris and Phil. They should do at least a couple of circuits of the room, each time jumping over Gladys as if she was a horse racing fence. On the final 'lap', everyone manages to tumble over Gladys and they all end up on the floor. At this point Gladys recovers from her faint, stands up and addresses the four actors who are now sitting up on the floor.)

GLADYS:
This building is a disaster. Pete – you don't build on sand because it's nice between your toes. Phil – you don't build on sand because you have a dream about it and Chris – you don't build on sand because it is easier. Houses built on sand are going to fall down and McDodgy, you should have known better. Let this be a lesson to you all!
(*Gladys walks off briskly. Pete gets to his feet, rescues his bag and checks his watch.*)

PETE:
Oops, I'm late. See you later!
(*McDodgy, Phil and Chris all gently get up.*)

MCDODGY:
Call yourself builders? The only building you'll ever manage will be out of Lego!

CHRIS:
How did he find out about that?

PHIL:
What?

CHRIS:
How did he know the only thing we really know how to build with is Lego!

MCDODGY:
The only thing you really know how to build with is Lego! Why didn't you tell me? Oh what a disaster – my reputation is ruined. All because of you two – come here!

PHIL:
Run!

CHRIS:
I suppose we should have built on rock!

MCDODGY:
Even a Lego builder should know that!

PHIL:
Run! (*McDodgy chases Chris and Phil off the stage and into the distance.*)

EPISODE B

SUMMARY: Phil and Chris eventually lose McDodgy. As they recover from the chase, they look back on the week's experiences. With the help of McDodgy, who manages to capture the boys halfway through the sketch, they again come to the conclusion that they should have built on rock.

PROPS: None.

TEACHING LINK: This sketch returns to the parable of the wise and foolish builders. The audience is left in no doubt that the only sensible place to build is on rock. The end of the sketch links directly back to Jesus' story.

(*Phil and Chris run to the front of the room, panting as if exhausted.*)

PHIL:
That's it, I can't run any more.

CHRIS:
Morning everyone. That's the longest chase scene I've ever been involved in! It started at... (*Fill in the time that Episode 5 ended on Day 5.*) on Friday!

PHIL:
It was a very long chase.

CHRIS:
(*Said, not chanted.*) Golden Palace – did we build it?

PHIL:
(*Said, not chanted.*) Golden Palace – yes we did! Well sort of!

CHRIS:
I hope we lost McPodgy.

PHIL:
That building contractor has never been called McPodgy!

CHRIS:
McPorky?

PHIL:
Nope, his name is McDodgy. Sir Robert McDodgy!

CHRIS:
Wasn't it funny when he asked us to build that massive palace for the King's birthday… all because he heard me asking you for my hotel back!

PHIL:
He didn't realise you were a Lego builder and not a real builder…

CHRIS:
And then, he promised to give us £500 each for building the Golden Palace in a week!

PHIL:
Yeah! Then we had to decide where to build it. We had the 'do we build it here' or 'do we build it here' issue.

CHRIS:
A very important one. Because 'here' was on sand and 'here' was on rock.

PHIL:
It was a very important decision. Do we build on sand or on rock?

CHRIS:
Building on rock would have been a lot harder…

PHIL:
But it would have had a solid foundation.

CHRIS:
Building on sand would have been quicker…

PHIL:
But it would have had a wobbly foundation.

CHRIS:
So which one did us clever builders choose?
(*They are so engrossed with their retelling of the story,*

that they don't notice Sir Robert McDodgy approaching from behind. He grabs them both by the ear.)

MCDODGY:
SAND!

CHRIS and PHIL:
Arrrghhhhh!

MCDODGY:
What should you have built my fantastic palace for the king on?

CHRIS and PHIL:
Rock, sir! We're very sorry, sir!

MCDODGY:
Yes! (*Letting Chris and Phil go, and turning very philosophical.*) Let this be a lesson to you. If you want to survive the storms of life, the shifting sands of uncertainty – if you are going to remain standing at the end of your little life, ready to take on the challenges of eternity – you need to listen to the instructions you're given and follow them!

CHRIS and PHIL:
Yeah! (*Not really following what McDodgy just said.*)

MCDODGY:
Hold on, that sounds good, that does. I'd better write that down. Instead of being a building contractor, I should become an author. I could write a book about building on rock and present that to the king. That's what I'll do! (*This line is said as he disappears off the stage.*)

PHIL:
Phew!

CHRIS:
What was that 'shifting sands of uncertainty' speech about then?

PHIL:
Listening to the right instructions and obeying them.

CHRIS:
Oh!

PHIL:
Hold on, when I was really small, Mum told me a story that Jesus told about builders – the wise and foolish builders – that was it. The wise one built on rock, and the stupid one built on sand. Jesus said that we would be like the wise man if we did what he said. The wise man obeyed the instructions that all builders are given – to build on rock.

CHRIS:
Oh yeah, Mum told me that one just a couple of weeks ago!

PHIL:
Then why didn't you remember it six days ago when this whole building episode began? You stupid banana! (*Exit, with Phil bashing Chris over the head in a friendly, brotherly sort of way.*)

THE WEATHER FORECAST

A team member puts on a silly wig, runs to the front and give a twenty-second weather forecast every morning. A script for this is included in each day's session outline. The weather forecaster is known as 'Heather on the Weather' and she will need an assistant who is responsible for operating the OHP and for responding to the weather forecast. When it rains, Heather gets squirted by a waterpistol, when it snows she gets covered in confetti, when it's windy she has a blow dry with a fan or hairdryer, and when it hails she has a bucket of ping-pong balls thrown over her! The scripts can be adapted and made as silly as you wish.

Equipment needed: OHP acetate with a map of your part of the world and weather symbols such as clouds and lightning; wig and jacket for Heather; waterpistol, bucket of confetti (or other snow-like substance), bucket of ping-pong balls, fan or hairdryer.

DANCING ON THE BEACH

One or two leaders lead the club in an aerobic warm-up each day. Ideally they should be dressed as aerobics instructors. You will need to choose a suitable dance track and play it loudly. It can be made particularly silly by acting as you dance. For example, on Day 2, you could mime building a house to the beat. Children can come and help with this later in the week.

Equipment: Sports kit, suitable dance track, PA/CD player.

PETER

Each day, the Bible story is either told by Peter via the *Seaside Rock* video, or by someone acting as Peter.

Suggested props: Peter costume, fishing net, rock, bag of sand, thermometer, bread, glass of wine and a fish (real if possible!)

LYN THE BIN

Lyn the Bin is a fun way of encouraging the children to contribute to *Seaside Rock*. Lyn the Bin has her own bin somewhere in the venue. Each day, the children are encouraged to bring in special mail for Lyn, such as jokes, pictures or stories. At some point between the beginning of the programme and Lyn's spot (twenty minutes or so before the end of the session), the team member who is playing Lyn will need to choose a few of the best contributions to share with the holiday club. Lyn is then given three or four minutes to perform.

Lyn works well if she is played by a man putting on a very high-pitched voice. She could have her own noticeboard to display the children's contributions. It is very easy for Lyn to get carried away, though, and take up too much time in the programme, so the Lifeguard will have to keep strict control!

For the costume, use a plastic dustbin with a head hole, arm holes and with its bottom cut out. Attach pieces of black bin-liner to the bottom to form a skirt. The actor needs to wear a long black wig, and black sweatshirt to make the arms black. The shoes should also be covered in bin-liner plastic.

IN FOR A SWIM!

This is a twenty-five minute activity section and it can be run in different ways.

Either every Rock Group does the same activity on the same day:

Pros – only one explanation from the front is needed, and group leaders can help each other. It also helps to develop relationships within the Rock Groups.

Cons – this requires a lot of resources, and activities which suit this format are limited.

Or a set of activities is set up for the week and children rotate around these activities:

Pros – fewer resources are need for each activity, more activities are possible, and different leaders can take responsibility for leading the same activity each day.

Cons – it is harder to theme each activity to the day's teaching. Some groups may not have their Rock Group leader with them during this time, if they are leading another activity. You will probably need specific areas which can be dedicated to each activity, and your venue may not be large enough.

The activities below are split into two categories: Beach Games and Beach Craft.

BEACH GAMES

1 COCONUT SHY

Aim: to knock as many cuddly toys as possible off a bench in five minutes.

Equipment: cuddly toys, set of beanbags (you might be able to borrow these from a local school), table or bench.

Rules: place the cuddly toys out along the table or bench and mark out a line about three metres away. Stand the children behind the line and give them the beanbags. On your signal, the children start to throw the beanbags at the cuddly toys to knock them off the bench. A leader behind the bench returns the beanbags. When all the toys have been knocked off, set them out again and continue the game. Each toy knocked off scores the team a point.

2 NEWSPRINT DESIGNER BEACHWEAR

Aim: to design, make and model the best designer beachwear.

Equipment: newspapers*, sticky tape and scissors.

Rules: briefly discuss beachwear with the children – go beyond swimming costumes to evening wear, T-shirts and more creative ideas! Give the children a pile of newspapers and tell them to design and make the best clothing they can. You will need a suitable amount of sticky tape for this manic fifteen minutes. The children should then show off their designs to each other and maybe the whole holiday club.

*The end of a newsprint roll can work even better, leaving no ink stains. These can usually be obtained from printers free or for a small fee.

3 PARACHUTE GAMES

Aim: to have loads of fun with a parachute.

Equipment: parachute (you may be able to borrow one from a local school or play centre), soft balls, whistle.

Rules: there are many different games you could play. Here are a couple of ideas:

a) Parachute football

Split the children into two teams, who then face each other over the parachute. Two leaders play the role of referee and assistant referee, and stand opposite each other in between the teams. Throw a soft ball on to the parachute. A team scores a goal when the ball flies off the parachute over the side of the opposing team. A goal is also conceded if the children handle the ball, although they are allowed to head it.

b) Sharks

The children sit around the edge of the parachute with their legs underneath the chute itself. A leader then nominates a few children to act as sharks. These children go under the parachute. The other children must try and roll soft balls (little fish) to one another under the parachute, while the sharks try and catch the little fish before they reach the other side. You could play in teams, one rolling the balls and the other being the sharks. Time how long it takes each team to catch all the little fish.

4 TIDAL WAVE

Aim: to stay out of the shark-infested rock pool by doing the actions that correspond with the commands shouted out by the leader.

Equipment: none.

Rules: one side of the room is designated the beach and the opposite side is the sea. On one of the other sides of the room a small area should be designated the 'shark-infested rock pool'. The game leader introduces a list of commands and demonstrates the actions which go with the commands. The children have to follow each command as quickly as possible. The last child to start doing an action is sent to have a swim in the 'shark-infested rock pool'. Children should be regularly allowed to join back in the game, eg after each 'Eight squid' is called. It is worth highlighting the need for sensible and thoughtful play.

Commands and actions

Tidal wave	Panic and run to the beach.
Whirlpool	All run round the sea in a circle.
Waves	Stand still with arms moving to signify a wave.
Coastguard	Sit with legs crossed, pretending to look through a pair of binoculars.
Surfers	Stand as if on a surfboard facing the beach, gently balancing on the waves.
Pirates	Stand on one leg, saluting with one hand, with one eye shut and shouting 'Arrrgh!'. Children should stay in this pose until the shout of 'Coastguard!', which frightens the pirates away. Children who move at decoy shouts could be sent to the shark-infested rock pool.
Sharks	Put one hand on top of head for fin, crouch and move slowly through the water.
Swim	Lie on the floor and pretend to swim.
Hurricane	Run out to sea very quickly.
Eight squid	Children quickly gather in groups of eight. Any children left out go to the shark-infested rock pool. (This action can be adapted, eg 'four squid' or 'six squid'.)

5 SHARKS

Aim: to survive being eaten by a shark!

Equipment: set of hoops (these could be borrowed from a local primary school), music, whistle.

Rules: appoint a couple of leaders or children to be sharks. Place the hoops around the room as 'bases'. The children should dance to the music (maybe gaining extra points for outrageous dancing), and avoiding the hoops. When the shout, 'Sharks are coming!' is given, the children should run into the safety of the nearest hoop. If a shark manages to tag a child before they reach a hoop, they are out. Gradually, the number of children playing is reduced until you have one or two winners. If you have different colour hoops, you can add an extra shout to warn that some are not safe – 'Sharks are coming, red's not safe!' for example. It is worth talking through with the children the need to be thoughtful and safe as they play.

6 OTHER GAMES

Some creative thinking around the seaside theme may well spark off some other fun games. Team relay races using a variety of equipment always go down well. The best games are often the ones where children are able to move and use up loads of energy whilst having fun.

BEACH CRAFTS

1 HAMA BEADS

Aim: to make a small coaster.

Equipment: Hama beads, boards (available from most toy shops), iron and ironing paper. (Hama beads are beads which melt together when heat is applied. The children's designs will become permanent when they are ironed.)

Activity: give out boards and boxes of beads to the children. Encourage them to make seaside designs by placing the beads carefully on their board. (You could provide templates to follow, although the children will probably come up with fantastic designs on their own!) When their design is complete, they should take the coaster carefully to the leader who is in charge of ironing the beads. (Be very careful when using an iron near children. Set up an area around the iron in which the children are not allowed to go.)

2 FISH SHAPES

Aim: to make a coloured fish out of card and tissue paper.

Equipment: simple card fish shape for each child (with the centre of the body and tail cut out so you are left with just the outline), tissue paper, scissors, felt-tip pens.

Activity: cut out a piece of tissue paper large enough to cover the body of the fish, and another to cover the tail. Stick these to the outline and then stick on smaller pieces of tissue paper for eyes and scales. Alternatively, use felt-tip pens to draw these on. To make a game, you could attach a paper clip to the mouth and try to catch the fish with a magnet on the end of a fishing line.

3 SEA MONSTERS

Aim: to create sea monsters out of clay.

Equipment: quick-drying clay, small pieces of card, small plastic bags.

Activity: help the children to create sea monsters with their piece of clay. Encourage them to be as imaginative as possible. When they have finished, put it inside a plastic bag with a labelled piece of card, to ensure that bits don't get lost when it is taken home.

4 MEXICAN STAR CROSS

Aim: to help the children talk about what happened when Jesus died on the cross.

Equipment: two drinking straws, kebab sticks or pieces of dowelling per child, sticky tape, different coloured wool.

Activity: show how to make the diamond pattern below, before encouraging the children to have a go themselves. Holding the end of the wool at the centre of the cross, pass the other end of the wool over one arm of the cross, round the back and then onto the next arm, pulling the yarn fairly tight as you go. Continue round the cross, changing colours as you go to make stripes. Tie the end of one colour to the start of another.

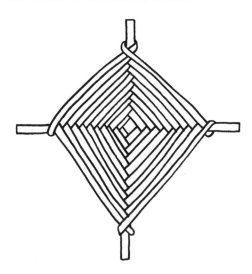

5 FISHING/BARBECUE COLLAGE

Aim: to make a collage appropriate to *Seaside Rock*.

Equipment: see below.

Activity: use netting, silver foil, coloured paper, lollipop sticks, wool, cotton wool and any other junk materials to make a fishing collage, either individually or as a group. This craft would particularly help reinforce the teaching from days 1 and 5.

6 SEASIDE MEMORY VERSE MOBILES

Aim: to make a seaside mobile.

Equipment: outlines of different seaside objects from the Beach Lookout pages, pens (see Part 7), glue, wire coat hangers, string, words of memory verses cut out (for younger children).

Activity: children can colour the shapes, and then stick the words of a memory verse on to each shape. These can then be hung from a coat hanger to make a mobile. Older children can cut their own shapes out and decorate them. They can also write the memory verse words onto the shapes before completing their mobile.

7 SEASIDE COOKIES

Aim: to decorate some seaside cookies.

Equipment: pre-cooked plain biscuits, decorations (different coloured icing, raisins, chocolate beans, cherries, chocolate chips etc.), plastic food bags.

Activity: ensure the children have clean hands, then give them one or two biscuits to decorate. They could try and make a seaside scene on their biscuits, and can take them home at the end of the day. (Be aware of food allergies. You can get wheat- and gluten-free products from many supermarkets, but be sensitive to children who still might not be able to take part.)

FAMILY SERVICE OUTLINE A

AIM: To introduce Peter and the key themes of *Seaside Rock*; to encourage the church to pray and be involved.

Key story: Peter is brought to Jesus by Andrew, an act that changed his life!

Key link to the holiday club: This week we will be bringing the children to Jesus, and children will be bringing their friends to Jesus.

Key passage: Peter is introduced to Jesus – John 1:35–42.

INTRODUCTION: The Llifeguard should give the church an overview of the aims and content of the week at *Seaside Rock*. The congregation should be encouraged to support the club through prayer.

Songs: Ask the Rock Band to introduce the *Seaside Rock* theme song.

DRAMA A: Meet Phil and Chris and discover why Day 1's sketch has a Lego hotel in it! (See pages 29 and 30.)

GAME: Beach Lookout (see page 9). Introduce the game to the congregation, using different pictures from all five days' material, as a link into the teaching theme.

PRAYER: Pray for the forthcoming holiday club. This could be done in various ways. Ask people to pray in small groups, or ask the team to come to the front of the church to be prayed for. Also pray for any children in the service who are coming. Their influence upon their friends who come is important.

Creative prayer idea: As you pray for the club, ask the congregation to write their names on a special 'Welcome to *Seaside Rock* from… ' acetate. Make sure this acetate is on the OHP each morning. This will help the children who come to *Seaside Rock* to understand that the whole church is behind the project.

STORY: Read the story of Andrew and Peter in John 1:35–42. A small group miming the content of this story as it is read will help bring the narrative to life.

TEACHING: Introduce Peter to the congregation, outlining his background and why Jesus chose him. (For a summary of Peter's life see page 78.) State that Peter was a very ordinary man, and yet his life was totally changed when he met Jesus – Jesus became his best friend and helped him to do wonderful things for God. Do not make too much of the name change, since that will feature in Day 1's material. It is significant, however, that Andrew and the other disciple found Jesus and then spent time with him, talking and listening. This is very much what we want children to do during *Seaside Rock*. Andrew then went to share what he had discovered with others, especially his brother – a very important action.

Looking forward to *Seaside Rock*, God is going to do some wonderful things through the adults and children who are taking part in the programme. Share some of the needs, asking the congregation to take time throughout the week to ask how things are going, to help out in a practical way, and to particularly watch out for the Lifeguard and any other key team members. Challenge the congregation: 'Have you been formally introduced to Jesus?' Is there someone else for whom God wants you to play the part of Andrew, by introducing them to Jesus? Encourage them to pray for *Seaside Rock* and to spread the word about what's going on to their friends and neighbours.

WORSHIP: Choose some songs which the congregation knows and worship God together.

Day 1: Peter, the Rock

AIMS FOR THE DAY:

To introduce Peter as the main character of the week, and to show how Jesus changed Peter's name because of his faith.

Peter: Peter introduces himself as Simon. He tells how Jesus called him to follow him, and eventually renamed him 'Rocky' or Peter.

Key story 1: Jesus calling Peter – Luke 5:1–11.

Key story 2: Peter's testimony – Matthew 16:13–20.

Key belief: Jesus loves everyone, even tough people like Peter!

TEAM PREPARATION

Spiritual preparation

Read together Luke 5:1–11; Matthew 16:13–20; John 1:42.

1 Talk together

Briefly discuss these questions:

o What was it about Peter that made Jesus choose him as one of his disciples?

o In what way was Peter like a child in his response to Jesus?

2 Share together

Peter was an ordinary man. You could say he was a surprising choice of disciple for Jesus to make. He was a streetwise fisherman, who had a fierce temper, but he also had a passionate heart and God-given leadership skills. Jesus would refine and channel these skills, making Peter the leader of his church.

Peter would probably have heard Jesus speaking before, but when Jesus called him to follow, he left immediately. Peter then spent the next three years eating, drinking and living with Jesus. When challenged in Matthew 16 as to who he thought Jesus was, Peter was the first to pronounce, 'You are the Son of the living God.' This belief is the cornerstone of the Christian faith – Christians down the centuries have lived and died for their belief that Jesus is the Son of God.

Today we are going to introduce the character of Peter to the children, focusing on his character and background. We will state what Peter believed and how it affected his life. We will then challenge the children as to what they believe about Jesus, and whether they are willing to let Jesus change them too.

3 Pray together

Pray for the day's activities.

Pray for the children as they are welcomed.

Pray for the team, that God will give you everything you need as you serve him today.

PRACTICAL PREPARATIONS

Talk through the morning's programme, and make sure everyone is aware of their responsibilities.

Encourage the team to be as welcoming and interactive with the children as possible. Remind them of Jesus' love for children, and how today they are going to begin to share this love with the children who come.

Ensure that all the resources are ready for the various activities.

Equipment checklist – Day 1

Security: registration forms, badges, pens, team lists.

Rock Groups: badges, pens, Bible, Rock Pool Challenge resources (A5 paper, glue, flip chart paper, felt-tip pens, scissors), postcards ready to be taken home at the end of the session, spare paper.

Music: background CD and music for the *Seaside Rock* song.

Drama: costumes and props.

Technology: check PA, OHP, video projector etc are working and in focus, check acetates for songs, *Seaside Rock* logo acetate, memory verse, Weather map and symbols, Beach Lookout and Mega Question.

Activities: all equipment needed for games and craft.

Lifeguard: running order, notes, Peter/Simon card for the teaching application, Rock Pool Challenge example on acetate.

Creative Prayer: flag.

Refreshments: drinks and biscuits.

Teaching: Peter costume, fishing net and rock or *Seaside Rock* video ready to play in the right place.

ROCK POOL WELCOME
(10 Minutes)

Rock Group time. Have some lively music playing on a CD player and the *Seaside Rock* logo on the OHP to welcome the children as they arrive and are registered. They are taken to their Rock Groups and introduced to their leader(s). Children can all make and decorate their name badges, if they are not using prepared ones. Group leaders should spend time getting to know the children. The Lifeguard should visit some of the Rock Groups to introduce themselves and chat. Team leaders should keep several name badges with them for late arrivals, as you go to the Seaside.

WELCOME TO THE SEASIDE!
(25 minutes)

LIFEGUARD WELCOME

The Lifeguard should end the Rock Group time and draw everyone's attention to the front. Welcome the children to *Seaside Rock*, and explain a little about the structure of the morning and the action-packed plans you have for the rest of the week.

WEATHER FORECAST

Lifeguard: Hello, Heather on the Weather. Can you give us the weather forecast for the beach today?

Heather: (*Bursting on to the stage, OHP with map is switched on. The following should be very quick and over the top.*) Indeed I can. Today is going to be a brilliant start to the week, with loads of sunshine (*Slap a couple of sun pictures on to the OHP.*) giving you lots of opportunity to have mega fun down on the beach. There might be a possibility of a short shower later in the day (*Water pistol is fired at Heather.*), but it's looking like a good day! Back to the studio! (*Heather leaves in a rush.*)

Lifeguard: Thank you, Heather!

DANCING ON THE BEACH

Choose a suitably bouncy piece of music, and get a couple of leaders to lead the children in an aerobic workout. This session should be made as active and as fun as possible. One of the aims of this is to use up a lot of energy!

BEACH LOOKOUT

The Lifeguard should quickly introduce the rules, before the children have a go at the game. The Lifeguard turns on the OHP for thirty seconds to show the day's acetate. The children have fifteen pictures to remember, all connected with today's story. In Rock Groups, the children are given ninety seconds to remember as many as possible. The Lifeguard reveals the pictures, one by one, with the Rock Group leaders marking their team's sheets. Award points for correct answers, if you are operating a points system. (Check out www.scriptureunion.org.uk/seasiderock for ideas on how to run a points system.)

THEME SONG

Teach the children the *Seaside Rock* theme song. Encourage the children to sing the words as best they can. Teach the children a suitably silly dance to go with it. This needs to have been made up beforehand – suggested actions are found on page 27.

PETER'S STORY – LIVE OR ON VIDEO

Either watch the first episode of the *Seaside Rock* video, or Peter appears on stage to tell his story.

Peter should use his body as much as possible to help tell the story, and should be carrying a fishing net and big rock. The following script is a guide, and can be adapted as suits your club.

Peter: Oh, hello. My name's Simon. Or Peter. Actually, I've got two names. When I was your age, I only had one – Simon. And even when I'd grown up and started to work as a fisherman, everyone called me Simon.

The first person to call me Peter was Jesus. It all started one exciting day when Jesus sat down in my boat. On that particular day, there were loads of people standing on the beach wanting to hear him speak. There were so many that Jesus got into my boat and used it like a stage. He started talking to everyone. When he'd finished telling us the most amazing things about God, Jesus turned to me and said, 'Simon, take your boat out into the lake and let down your nets.' Well, we usually fished at night because that's when it's easiest to catch fish, but I did what he said. We rowed out into the lake and let down our nets. The funny thing was that the night before we'd caught absolutely nothing. Then suddenly – an amazing thing happened. Our nets were bursting with tons of fish. I fell on my knees before him. Who was this man? Jesus whispered to me, 'Simon, follow me', so I did.

While I was travelling with him, I saw Jesus do loads of other amazing things, like control the weather, bring dead people back to life and heal the sick.

Then came the day when Jesus changed my name. He asked me and the rest of his disciples, 'Who do people think I am?' So we told him that some people had strange ideas about him.

Then Jesus asked us, 'Who do you think I am?' Well, I knew, so I told him.

'Lord, you're the Messiah, the Son of the living God!' And do you know what he did – he smiled, 'cos I'd got it right! Then he changed my name to Peter, which means 'Rock'. Jesus said that believing he was the Son of God is very important… like having a massive rock that you can build your house on. He said he was going to build his group of followers on what I believed! Anyway, even though the rest of the lads realised it was an important name, they used to tease me a bit, calling me Rocky…

I'll see you tomorrow!

TEACHING APPLICATION

Use the following points to talk about Peter's story, making very clear the main points that Peter made.

Props: A sheet of card with 'Simon – the Fisherman' on one side and 'Peter – the Rock' on the other.

In the story, Peter tells us he was known by two names:

1) (*Hold up the card with 'Simon – the Fisherman' on it.*) Firstly, the name his parents gave him was Simon. Simon was an ordinary man, just like you and me. He was a fisherman, who sometimes got really angry and sometimes said things he shouldn't have done. Do you ever get angry or say things you shouldn't? That day, when Jesus stood in his boat, Simon decided to follow Jesus. I wonder if you've ever thought about following Jesus. Maybe you don't know much about him. This week at *Seaside Rock*, we'll find out loads about him, and you'll be able to decide for yourselves if you want to follow him!

2) Peter told us that Jesus changed his name. Jesus gave him a new name, a nickname if you like, because of what he believed. (*Turn the card around to reveal 'Peter – the Rock' written on the back.*)

Peter believed that Jesus was the Son of God. Jesus was God living as a man! What Peter said must have been very important to Jesus. I wonder what you believe about Jesus? Over the rest of the week, we're going to find out why Peter believed that Jesus was the Son of God!

HOLIDAY SNAPSHOTS

Today's memory verse:

> Simon Peter spoke up, 'You are the Messiah, the Son of the living God!'
> Matthew 16:16

Read this first from the Bible to make it clear where the verse comes from. See pages 25 and 26 for some creative ideas on how to use memory verses, including information on the memory verse song, along with suggested actions, for each day. The words used in the memory verse song are a paraphrase.

ROCK POOL CHALLENGE
(10 minutes)

For all age groups, slowly read Luke 5:1–11. Before you do so, give each child a piece of coloured paper and a felt-tip pen. Ask them to doodle as they listen. Suggest that they might draw a boat, the sea, a seagull or something that they hear in the story. Then, using these pictures as decoration, challenge each group to make a poster of their names. Give each child a piece of A5 paper. Ask them to draw and decorate their names and put a small picture next to it – a picture of something that means a lot to them. (Ideally the Lifeguard should draw and decorate their own name onto an acetate. This can be shown on the OHP as an example.) Peter might have drawn a picture of Jesus, or of his fishing boat. As they do this, ask the children what their own names mean and why they have nicknames. Discuss the significance of Peter's change of name. (It might be interesting for the children if you have a dictionary of names and their meanings. You would then be able to check out what each of their names mean.)

Rock Group leaders should cut out the names and pictures and put them onto a big sheet of paper, which can then be stuck up on the wall near the Rock Pool. (This will need to be done after the children have left at the end of the morning, ready for Day 2.)

REFRESHMENT KIOSK

(5 minutes)

Drinks as the children go to activities.

IN FOR A SWIM!

(25 minutes)

Beach Games and Beach Crafts (see page 42).

LET'S GO SUNBATHE!

(40 minutes)

MEGA QUESTION

Put today's Mega Question on the OHP – 'Who would you most like to invite to tea?'

Ask a few people for their answers to the Mega Question, and finish by stating that Peter ate lots of meals with Jesus, and became really close friends with him. His answer to the Mega Question would probably be 'Jesus'. Jesus is very special, and Peter must have got to know him really well. We'll hear more from Peter tomorrow!

SONG

Either sing the **Seaside Rock** theme song or introduce another song to the children.

LYN THE BIN

Introduce Lyn the Bin to everyone. Lyn should tell a few suitable silly jokes and encourage the children to bring in some jokes and pictures for her. The children should put their name and group on their piece of paper, and put it in Lyn's special bin when they arrive tomorrow morning!

MEMORY JOGGER

Ask the children what they can remember of today's programme, including the memory verse.

DRAMA

See today's script on page 30.

CREATIVE PRAYER

Encourage the children with the knowledge that God knows their name and that God can hear lots of people talking at the same time. Say that you are going to pray together. One leader should be ready with a flag, or some other object they can hold up easily at the right moment. The Lifeguard (or another leader) then reads the prayer outlined below. Every time the flag is raised, the children shout their name to God in the prayer! Don't read the prayer too slowly.

Dear Lord,

It's *(flag)* here.

Thank you that I, *(flag)* could come to **Seaside Rock** today.

Thank you for all the fun that I, *(flag)*, have had. Please help me, *(flag)*, to learn loads, and to have a great time tomorrow too.

Amen

THEME SONG

Sing the theme song once more to bring an end to today's programme.

ROCK POOL GROUPS

(5 minutes)

Give the children today's postcard, and encourage them to complete the activities on it at home. They might like to bring it back tomorrow. Children should collect their belongings ready for departure. Make sure that each child is collected by the appropriate adult.

Memory verse:

Simon Peter spoke up, "You are the Messiah, the Son of the living God."

Matthew 16:16

Seaside
DAY 1
Rock

Write your name in bubble writing and decorate it with seaside things, like a crab, seaweed or an ice-cream.

In today's story, Jesus called Simon the fisherman to become one of his followers or disciples. He gave Simon a new name, Peter, which means 'the Rock'. Jesus wants all of us to be his followers, too.

DAY 1'S MEGA WORDSEARCH

J	A	M	E	S	E	R	O	H	S
K	N	E	L	T	F	K	N	S	E
C	A	T	C	H	C	H	O	I	A
L	H	L	A	O	O	J	B	F	S
D	O	R	R	J	W	E	O	S	I
L	R	N	I	A	P	S	A	A	D
I	E	O	M	S	E	U	T	N	E
U	N	M	N	E	T	S	S	D	R
B	N	I	E	B	E	A	C	H	O
F	I	S	H	E	R	M	E	N	C
D	S	L	O	O	K	O	U	T	K

beach
boats
build
catch
Christ
fish
fishermen
James
Jesus
John
knelt
lookout
miracle
nets
Peter
rock
sand
sea
Seaside Rock
shore
Simon
sinner

Use the spare letters to see what Peter did.
Peter _____ Jesus

Beach Lookout Day 1

M

Mega Question

Who would you most
like to invite to tea?

Day 2: The wise and foolish builders

AIMS FOR THE DAY:

To tell the story of the wise and foolish builders and apply it to the children's lives and to show the children they are loved by Jesus.

Peter: Peter introduces his house and retells the story of the wise and foolish builders (briefly outlining some of Jesus' practical teaching about anger and bad words from the Sermon on the Mount – two things close to Peter's experience).

Key story: The wise and foolish builders – Matthew 7:24–27. Note: Peter's experience of walking on water is tied in to this parable – Matthew 14:22–32.

Key belief: Jesus wants us to listen to him and obey.

TEAM PREPARATION

Spiritual preparation

Read together Matthew 7:24–27 and 14:22–32.

1 Talk together

Briefly discuss these questions:

o What was the difference between the wise and the foolish man?

o Spend five minutes in small groups skim-reading the Sermon on the Mount, jotting down Jesus' commands when you find them. Then spend a few moments reflecting on what you discover. How do your lives match up?

2 Share together

Peter would have spent many hours sitting at Jesus' feet (teachers in Jesus' time would have sat down to teach). He would have gazed up into Jesus' eyes, transfixed by every word he said. Jesus' words about controlling anger and swearing from the Sermon on the Mount would have been a challenge to Peter. Jesus was setting a very practical challenge to his disciples for Godly living.

It's important to note that everyone heard what Jesus had to say, but only the wise did what Jesus commanded.

Talk about the ways in which Peter might have responded to Jesus when he saw Jesus walking on the water. How was he putting Jesus' words into action?

Are we like the wise or the foolish man? Does the evidence of our lives reflect the teachings of Jesus? Today we are going to challenge ourselves and the children to listen to the words of Jesus and to put them into practice, just like Peter did!

3 Pray together

Pray for the conversations with parents as they bring and pick up their children.

Pray that the children have a great time at **Seaside Rock** today.

Pray that the children will hear and understand the teaching of Jesus.

Pray for the team, that God will enable them to work together really well as they serve him.

PRACTICAL PREPARATIONS

Talk through the morning's programme, and make sure everyone is aware of their responsibilities.

Encourage the team to be as welcoming and interactive with the children as possible. Encourage them to particularly look out for any new children today and to help them settle into their group and the programme. Encourage the team to motivate their Rock Groups to listen and join in.

Ensure that all the resources are ready for the various activities.

Equipment checklist – Day 2

Security: registration forms, badges, pens, team lists.

Rock Groups: badges, pens, Bible, Rock Pool Challenge resources (flip chart, pens, Bibles or printed copies of Matthew 5:38 – 6:15), creative prayer resources (bricks made from brown sugar paper, pens), postcards ready to be taken home at the end of the session, spare paper.

Music: background CD and music for the *Seaside Rock* song. On Dave Godfrey's album, *Heaven's No. 1*, there is an appropriate song, *Ace Foundations*, about the wise and foolish builders. (This song is also a bonus track on the *Seaside Rock* single.)

Drama: costumes and props ready.

Technology: check PA, OHP, video projector etc are working and in focus, check acetates for songs, *Seaside Rock* logo acetate, Weather map and symbols, Beach Lookout, memory verse and Mega Question.

Activities: all equipment needed for games and craft.

Lifeguard: running order, notes, pictures of the two buildings on card, two cards with the word 'listen' and one card with the word 'obey' to use as visual aids.

Refreshments: drinks and biscuits.

Teaching: Peter costume, bag of sand and rock, or *Seaside Rock* video ready to play in the right place.

ROCK POOL WELCOME
(10 Minutes)

Rock Group time

Play some lively music on a CD player and put the *Seaside Rock* logo on the OHP to welcome the children as they arrive and are registered. They should join their Rock Groups. Any children bringing jokes or pictures for Lyn the Bin should place them in her special bin. If there's time, challenge the children to remember yesterday's memory verse. New children need to be given a badge.

WELCOME TO THE SEASIDE!
(25 minutes)

LIFEGUARD WELCOME

The Lifeguard should end the Rock Group time and draw everyone's attention to the front. Welcome the children to Day 2 of *Seaside Rock* and explain the structure the morning for those who are new today. Conclude this section with the weather forecast.

WEATHER FORECAST

Lifeguard: Hello, Heather on the Weather. Can you give us the weather for the beach today?

Heather: (*Bursts on to the stage and picks up the fan which is hiding behind the OHP. The OHP with map is switched on by assistant.*) Indeed I can. Today is going to be a bit windy! (*Assistant puts wind pictures on screen, Heather switches on the fan to maximum, facing it.*) There will still be loads of fun down on the beach, however. Later in the day, the wind will die down (*Turn off fan.*) with a slight chance of short showers! (*Waterpistol is fired at Heather.*) That's it from me – I'll be back tomorrow. Bye! (*Heather leaves in a huge rush.*)

Lifeguard: Thank you, Heather!

DANCING ON THE BEACH

Play a suitably bouncy piece of music while a couple of leaders lead the children in an aerobic workout. Do some building actions to the song, whilst making it as energetic as possible.

BEACH LOOKOUT

Explain the rules to the children as described on page 9, and then play the game!

THEME SONG

Remind the children of the actions to the song if necessary.

PETER'S STORY – LIVE OR ON VIDEO

Either watch the second episode of the *Seaside Rock* video, or introduce Peter live on stage to tell his story: .

Peter should be suitably dressed and should be carrying a bag of sand and the rock used in Day 1.

Oh, hello again. It's Simon. Or Peter… I told you all about my names yesterday. You can call me Peter.

I loved to listen to Jesus' stories – he was great at telling them. Each one had a meaning behind it. Every time Jesus told a story, I used to think, 'What's the hidden meaning?'

Anyway, one day Jesus took his disciples, and anyone else who wanted to listen, up the side of a hill. He sat down on a rock. I sat at his feet and looked straight up into his eyes. He smiled at me, and then he started speaking. He taught us how to pray and how we should act. Some of the things he said were really difficult to follow. I've always had a strong temper, and if someone used to hurt me, I'd thump them… But Jesus said, 'If someone hits you, don't hit them back. Love the people who hurt you!' Then he started talking about the words we say. Sometimes I can say some really bad things, but Jesus told me to only let good things come out of my mouth.

Then he started telling this story. He said there were once two builders. One of them decided to build his house on rock, so that when the wind and the rain came and the river flooded, the house was OK. The other built his house on sand, though, and when the wind and the rain came and the river flooded, his house fell down. What a stupid man, I thought. Of course you don't build your house on sand! Then I thought, 'Why did Jesus tell that story?' This time, Jesus told us what the story meant. He said 'Anyone who hears and obeys these teachings of mine is like a wise person who built a house on solid rock… And anyone who hears my teachings and doesn't obey them is like a foolish man who built on sand.'

I decided right there and then, while I was sitting at his feet, that I want to build my life on rock and do everything that Jesus tells me to do! Oops, gotta go – I can feel a storm coming along! See you tomorrow… Bye!

Note: *If you watch the video for Day 2 you will see that the story of the wise and foolish builders has been linked to the story of Peter walking on water. You may wish to incorporate this story into the script above – Peter heard what Jesus said and he obeyed him. But when he stopped trusting, he got into trouble.*

TEACHING APPLICATION

Use the following points to reinforce the story of the wise and foolish builders:

Props: Pictures of the two buildings on card, two cards with the word 'listen' and one card with the word 'obey' to use as visual aids.

Ask the children this question: 'What material did the two builders build on in Jesus' story?' (As the two buildings are mentioned, ask two children to come and hold the pictures for you.)

1) Jesus was an excellent storyteller. Both men in the story we have just heard were building a house. Jesus said that the people who listen to him and obey him are like the wise man who built on rock. He also said that the people who listen to him and do not obey him are like the foolish man who built on sand. What do both sorts of people do? The answer is that they both listen to what Jesus says. (*Ask two more children to come and hold the two 'listen' words, one next to each house.*) Lots of people don't know what Jesus has said because they have never listened to his stories or read the Bible. I'm really glad you're here to listen this week!

2) If one house is the wise man's and the other house is the foolish man's, what did the wise man do in the story, that the foolish man didn't? The wise man built on **rock**, which was the best thing to do! If both wise and foolish people listen to what Jesus says, what do only the wise people do? The answer is that they **obey**, which is also the best thing to do! (*Ask one more child to come and stand next to the wise man's house to hold the card entitled 'obey'. Add some personal testimony here about what you have discovered as you have done what Jesus said.*) Peter decided not just to listen to Jesus, but to obey him. Do you think that was the wisest thing for him to do?

HOLIDAY SNAPSHOTS

Today's memory verse:

> Jesus said, 'Anyone who hears and obeys these teachings of mine is like a wise person who built a house on solid rock.' **Matthew 7:24**

First of all, read this from the Bible to show where it comes from. See pages 25 and 26 for some creative ideas on how to use memory verses, including information on the memory verse song, along with suggested actions, for each day. The words used in the memory verse song are a paraphrase.

ROCK POOL CHALLENGE
(10 minutes)

If you used the video, discuss how Peter's feelings changed. Draw a series of blank faces on flip chart paper, and ask the children to fill them in. How did Peter show he was listening to Jesus? Read Matthew 14:22–32 to the children.

On another piece of flip chart paper, draw a house on rock at the top of the sheet, and a house on sand at the bottom. Reinforce the story that Peter told about the wise and foolish builders, and what Jesus meant. In the house built on sand, write the opposite of some of the things Jesus said we should do, for example, ignore what he says, hate our enemies, hit someone when they hit you, call people names, ignore God, do bad things (all from the Sermon on the Mount). Discuss with the children what we should do if we want to be like the wise man. Record their answers in the house on rock. Discuss how easy or hard it is to do the wise things. Encourage the children that God promises to help and he wants us to make wise choices!

With junior-aged children, hand out Bibles or printed copies of Matthew 5:38 – 6:15 with these verses highlighted 5:39,42,44,48; 6:1,3,5,6,14. Ask the children to check out that Jesus really did say some of the things you have written down. With younger children, read Luke 7:24–27 and ask them to work out actions to go with the reading, such as rain coming down.

REFRESHMENT KIOSK
(5 minutes)

Drinks as the children go to activities.

IN FOR A SWIM!
(25 minutes)

Beach Games and Beach Crafts (see page 42).

LET'S GO SUNBATHE!
(40 minutes)

MEGA QUESTION

Put today's Mega Question on the OHP – 'What are the wobbliest things you can stand on?'

Ask a few children/leaders for their answers to the Mega Question, and finish by stating that Peter listened carefully to all that Jesus said and he obeyed him, which included walking on the water. Living for Jesus is not an easy option, but God promises that he will help us.

SONG

Either the **Seaside Rock** theme song, or introduce another song to the children. You could go back over yesterday's memory verse song.

LYN THE BIN

Invite Lyn the Bin on to the stage. She should read out some jokes and show some pictures (chosen from those brought by the children), making witty, encouraging comments and awarding points. Lyn should encourage the children to bring in some jokes and pictures tomorrow. Remind the children that they should put their name and group on their piece of paper, and put them in Lyn's special bin when they arrive in the morning.

MEMORY JOGGER

Ask the children what they can remember of today's programme, including the memory verse.

DRAMA

See today's script on page 32.

CREATIVE PRAYER

Hand out a piece of brown sugar paper to each child, cut into the shape of a brick. Encourage them to write a short prayer, asking God to help them do something that they find difficult, for example, loving people who don't love them. The younger ones can draw a picture. Whilst the children are drawing and writing, the Lifeguard should pray over the children on their behalf, asking for God's help and wisdom. The bricks should be collected and built into a wall of prayer. This can be done when the children have gone home.

THEME SONG

Sing the theme song once more to bring an end to today's programme.

ROCK POOL GROUPS
(5 minutes)

Give the children today's postcard, and encourage them to complete the activities on it at home. They might like to bring it back tomorrow. Children should collect their belongings ready for departure. Ensure that each child is collected by the appropriate adult.

Memory verse:

Jesus said, "Anyone who hears and obeys these teachings of mine is like a wise person who built a house on solid rock."

Matthew 7:24

Seaside DAY 2 Rock

DAY 2'S MEGA SPOT THE DIFFERENCE PUZZLE

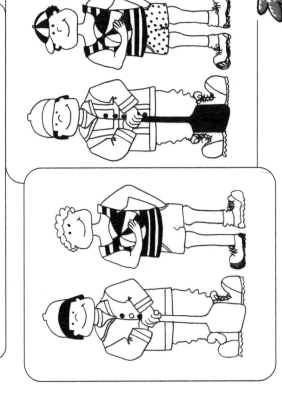

Write down your favourite joke to share with others at *Seaside Rock*.

Jesus told a story about two builders. One did the right thing and built his house on rock. The other did the wrong thing and built on sand. Jesus said that people who listen to him and do what he says are wise people.

How many differences can you spot?

Beach Lookout Day 2

Mega Question
What are the wobbliest things you can stand on?

Day 3: Jesus heals Peter's mother-in-law

AIMS FOR THE DAY:

To tell the story of Jesus healing Peter's mother-in-law, and to show that Jesus, the Son of God, has the power to heal and that he loves families.

Peter: Peter tells how Jesus came to his house to see his mother-in-law and healed her. (Peter also relates one or two other miracles that convince him of who Jesus is.)

Key story: The healing of Peter's mother-in-law – Matthew 8:14,15.

Key belief: Jesus is powerful and he is interested in ordinary families.

TEAM PREPARATION

Spiritual preparation

Read together Matthew 8:14–17; Luke 4:38–41.

1 Talk together

Briefly discuss these questions:

o Why do we sometimes find it easier keeping Jesus out of our everyday lives?

o What effect do you think Jesus wants to have on the life of our family?

2 Share together

What a wonderful story! In it Jesus demonstrates his love for an ordinary family. Jesus went to the house of Peter because of his love and concern for a woman – Peter's mother-in-law. Imagine the family's joy as Jesus dramatically tells the fever to go and Peter's mother-in-law gets up fit and well.

The news spread fast! After sunset many people, having heard what Jesus did, brought sick and demon-possessed people to Jesus. Luke tells us he healed them all, and that Jesus had to silence the demons (Luke 4:41). As spiritual beings, they knew exactly who Jesus was. This was in contrast to Peter – he needed a revelation from God the Father, as we saw in Day 1. Here, Jesus orders the demons to come out and to be quiet.

In today's programme, we want the children to once again understand who Jesus is and to realise that he cares for ordinary families like theirs.

3 Pray together

Pray for the developing relationships with the children and their families.

Pray for the children to have a great time again today at **Seaside Rock**.

Pray that the children will grasp the concept that Jesus is the Son of God, and that he cares for them and their families.

Pray for the team, that God will help them today to have some top-quality conversations with the children.

PRACTICAL PREPARATIONS

Talk through the morning's programme, and make sure everyone is aware of their responsibilities.

Encourage the team to be as welcoming and interactive with the children as possible, and to keep up the momentum gained over the last couple of days. Encourage them also to enjoy their relationships with the children and to use every opportunity to get to know them.

Ensure that all resources are ready for the various activities.

Equipment checklist – Day 3

Security: registration forms, badges, pens, team lists.

Rock Groups: badges, pens, Bible, Rock Pool Challenge resources (flip chart paper, pens and Bibles or copies of John 14), creative prayer resources (plastic sticky plaster per child, red cardboard heart, pens), postcards ready to be taken home at the end of the session, spare paper.

Music: background CD and music for the **Seaside Rock** song.

Drama: costumes and props.

Technology: check PA, OHP, video projector etc are working and in focus, check acetates for songs, *Seaside Rock* logo acetate, Weather map and symbols, Beach Lookout, memory verse and Mega Question.

Activities: all equipment needed for games and craft.

Lifeguard: running order, notes, family photograph and bandage for the teaching application.

Refreshments: drinks and biscuits.

Teaching: Peter costume and thermometer, or *Seaside Rock* video ready to play in the right place.

ROCK POOL WELCOME
(10 Minutes)
Rock Group time

Play some lively music on a CD player and put the *Seaside Rock* logo on an OHP to welcome the children as they arrive and are registered. They should join their Rock Groups. Any children bringing jokes or pictures for Lyn the Bin should place them in her special bin. If there's time, challenge the children to remember the memory verses from the last two days.

WELCOME TO THE SEASIDE!
(25 minutes)

LIFEGUARD WELCOME

The Lifeguard should end the Rock Group time, and draw everyone's attention to the front. Welcome the children to Day 3 of *Seaside Rock*, and explain the structure of the morning for those who are new.

WEATHER FORECAST

Lifeguard: Hello, Heather on the Weather. Can you give us the weather for the beach today?

Heather: (*Bursting on to the stage, having previously splashed her face with water. The OHP with map is switched on by assistant.*) Indeed I can. Today is going to be really, really hot! (*Assistant puts massive sun pictures on screen, Heather wipes her sweat-soaked brow, flicking some water over the children near her!*) I'm sure there will be loads of fun down there on the beach, but I'm gonna need a shower to cool me down. (*Waterpistol is fired at Heather.*) I'll be back tomorrow. Bye! (*Heather leaves in a rush.*)

Lifeguard: Thank you, Heather!

DANCING ON THE BEACH

Play a suitably bouncy piece of music while a couple of leaders lead the children in an aerobic workout. Do some nursing actions to the song (to fit in with the story for today) whilst making it as energetic as possible!

BEACH LOOKOUT

Explain the rules to the children, and then play the game!

THEME SONG

Sing the theme song once together.

PETER'S STORY – LIVE OR ON VIDEO

Either watch the third episode of the *Seaside Rock* video, or have Peter arrive live on stage to tell his story.

Peter should be suitably dressed and carrying a thermometer.

Oh, hello! It's me again, Peter.

Can you remember the memory verse from two days ago? (*Pause for audience participation.*) Well, when I look back on it, there was one special day that really helped me to understand who Jesus was and is.

That day, I was out with Jesus, when suddenly I got this urgent message – 'Come home now!' I left Jesus and the other disciples, and ran home as quickly as I could. When I got home, my wife was in tears. I had to calm her down. 'What's wrong?' I asked.

She said, 'It's Mum!' I dashed into the bedroom, and there on the bed was my wife's mum. She looked terrible. I went closer – she was very, very hot and in a lot of pain. I knew what to do immediately. I sprinted out of the house and back to Jesus. I said to him, 'Lord, please come back to my house. My mother-in-law is dying. Please help.' Jesus came back with me, and I took him into the bedroom. (*Pause.*)

Jesus spoke gently to Mum, and then did something I wasn't expecting. In a loud voice, he said, 'Fever, I command you to go!' Immediately, the fever left my mother-in-law. She was healed. She got up and went to put the kettle on. It was amazing! Then it struck me – Jesus really cared for my family. I hadn't thought about it before!

Everyone was amazed at what happened, and they told their friends. In fact the news of what Jesus did spread really quickly. By the time evening came, loads of people had brought their poorly and sick friends around to my house to see Jesus. Jesus spoke to each one in turn, and then healed them of broken arms and legs, cuts and bruises, headaches, skin problems, fevers, internal problems, even the blind and those who couldn't walk… everyone got healed!

The day that Jesus came round to my house was a special day, made special by Jesus, the Son of God. The other thing I quickly realised was that whenever I needed help, Jesus would always be there! Even when there was trouble at home with my family!

Gotta go… Bye!

TEACHING APPLICATION

Ask the children some questions, eg 'Who was it that Jesus healed?'

This story tells us two things:

1) Jesus is someone very special. (*Invite a child to come and help you, then begin putting a bandage around his head and shoulders, pausing to tell the children about each miracle.*) Peter saw Jesus do some amazing things. He once told a storm to stop, and it did. He once fed 5000 people from one packed lunch. He healed a man who was totally blind and he even brought a little girl back to life! On the day Jesus went to Peter's house loads of people came to him who were sick. Only Jesus had the power to heal everyone. Peter knew that whenever he needed help, Jesus was there for him. The same is true today. Peter saw how powerful Jesus was and gradually came to understand that Jesus was God living as a human being. (*Suddenly take off the bandage.*) On the day the story happened, you wouldn't have needed many of these! (*Give the bandage to the child and ask him to rejoin his group and take the bandage away.*)

2) Although Jesus is so amazing and powerful, he still cares for ordinary families. (*Hold up a family photograph.*) He came to Peter's house and healed his mother-in-law. Jesus cared for and loved everyone he met. Jesus is now alive in heaven, and he knows all about us and loves us, and that goes for everyone in our families – which is great! (*If it is appropriate, you may want to talk about the Holy Spirit and his role in our lives.*)

HOLIDAY SNAPSHOTS

Today's memory verse:

> With only a word Jesus forced out the evil spirits and healed everyone who was sick.
> Matthew 8:16

First of all, read this from the Bible to show where it comes from. See pages 25 and 26 for some creative ideas on how to use memory verses, including information on the memory verse song, along with suggested actions, for each day. The words used in the memory verse song are a paraphrase.

You may want to explain to the children that, at the time of Jesus, people did not have the understanding of medical science that we do now. Many illnesses were understood in terms of someone being possessed or influenced in some way by an evil spirit. While this was (and is) occasionally true and Jesus had to rebuke a demon, for example, in Matthew 8:28–34, on the whole, people suffered illnesses just as we do. The important thing is that Jesus was (and is) able to heal people in a very simple and straightforward way.

ROCK POOL CHALLENGE
(10 minutes)

Gather the children around a sheet of flip chart paper. As a group, imagine Jesus was coming round to your house – how would you prepare for his visit? How would you make him feel welcome? Record these answers on your sheet.

With older children, find John 14:25,26. Either make sure each child has a Bible or copy of John 14. Put the first part of John 14:25 in code for the children to work out, and then check what the rest of the two verses say in their Bibles. With younger children, read Luke 4:38,39 and ask them to act out the story as a group.

Even though we can't see Jesus, he is at home with us and our family. Jesus went to heaven and in his place, the Holy Spirit came. That now means that God, in the form of the Holy Spirit, is here with us now. What can we do to show him that we love him? (Record these answers on your sheet.)

REFRESHMENT KIOSK
(5 minutes)

Drinks as the children go to activities.

IN FOR A SWIM!
(25 minutes)

Beach Games and Beach Crafts (see page 42).

LET'S GO SUNBATHE!
(40 minutes)

MEGA QUESTION

Put today's Mega Question on the OHP – 'In your group, who has got the oldest and the youngest person living in their home?'

The Lifeguard can ask a few children/leaders for their answers to the Mega Question and finish by stating that Peter once had Jesus come to his home. Peter learnt that Jesus cared for his family, and that Jesus was very special because he was able to heal people. This helped Peter to understand that Jesus is the Son of God.

SONG

Either sing the **Seaside Rock** theme song or introduce another song to the children. You could recap the previous days' memory verse songs.

LYN THE BIN

Invite Lyn the Bin on to the stage. She should read out some jokes and show some pictures (chosen from those brought by the children), making witty, encouraging comments and awarding points. Lyn should encourage the children to bring in some jokes and pictures tomorrow. Remind the children that they should put their name and group on their piece of paper, and put them in Lyn's special bin when they arrive in the morning.

MEMORY JOGGER

Ask the children what they can remember of today's programme, including the memory verse.

DRAMA

See today's script on page 34.

CREATIVE PRAYER

Ask the children to think of someone they know who is not feeling very well. Encourage them that Jesus is alive and with us, even though we cannot see him. Peter told Jesus about his poorly mother-in-law – we can also tell Jesus about someone we know who is sick. We can ask Jesus to make them better. Give each child a plastic sticking plaster. Ask them, or help them, to write down the name of the sick person they want to pray for on the plaster. The children can stick this on to the Rock Group's cardboard heart – as a way of asking a loving God to heal them. (For smaller clubs, one big heart could be used by everyone.)

Note: *For some children, this is a very significant issue. They may have a disability or a chronically ill or dying grandparent. Jesus can heal and restore anyone today, but he may not do so. We need to encourage the child to pray with faith, trusting that God knows best.*

THEME SONG

Sing the theme song once more to bring an end to today's programme.

ROCK POOL GROUPS
(5 minutes)

Give the children today's postcard, and encourage them to complete the activities on it at home. They might like to bring it back tomorrow. Children should collect their belongings ready for departure. Ensure each child leaves with the appropriate adult.

Memory verse:
With only a word Jesus forced out the evil spirits and healed everyone who was sick.
Matthew 8:16

Seaside
DAY 3
Rock

Write down the name of someone you know who is ill or in need. Pray for them now!

In today's story, Jesus healed Peter's mother-in-law who was very sick. Jesus showed just how powerful he is and how much he cares for families.

DAY 3'S MEGA WORDSEARCH

S	T	I	R	I	P	S	L	I	V	E	W	G	R	H
Z	J	F	M	G	N	I	Z	A	M	A	D	E	A	F
W	G	S	B	L	F	O	B	P	L	G	V	N	F	V
M	A	N	J	E	S	U	S	N	Z	E	D	G	X	P
P	W	S	I	C	K	E	I	Q	F	D	N	I	L	B
J	E	G	N	R	R	X	P	A	I	N	M	E	L	
I	H	V	N	V	E	A	T	H	L	S	F	X	P	K
T	T	E	E	H	I	V	E	A	F	A	O	U	W	G
U	T	O	T	R	E	T	E	P	E	E	M	Q	V	A
F	A	O	U	O	S	H	N	P	M	S	Z	E	T	K
F	M	U	V	C	O	E	F	Y	O	J	G	U	N	C
F	B	R	K	K	H	V	P	J	S	N	X	W	S	W

amazing
blind
deaf
eight
evening
evil spirits
fever
hand
happy
healing
Jesus
joy
lame
Matthew
mother
-in-law
pain
Peter
rock
seaside
serve
sick
sixteen
touch
verse

Beach Lookout Day 3

Day 4: Peter and the cross

AIMS FOR THE DAY:

To tell the story of Peter's denial and Jesus' death, and to show that Jesus' death makes it possible for our sin, to be forgiven.

Peter: Peter tells of his denial and Jesus' crucifixion using the symbols of bread and wine – Peter relates how he really let Jesus down, and how Jesus died to forgive him!

Key story 1: The Last Supper – Mark 14:12–26.

Key story 2: Peter and the cross of Jesus – Matthew 26:31–35,58,69–75.

Key belief: We let Jesus down, just like Peter did. Jesus died so that we can be forgiven and know God as our special friend.

TEAM PREPARATION

Spiritual preparation

Read together Matthew 26:17–35,58,69–75

1 Talk together

Briefly discuss these questions:

o   To what extent do you think the disciples understood the significance of the bread and the wine as Jesus was speaking?

o   In what ways did Peter's feelings and emotions change through the events of Matthew 26 and subsequently?

2 Share together

We've probably all felt bad when we've let someone down whom we love. Peter must have felt terrible when the cock crowed. All the time and effort, all the love and encouragement of Jesus seemed to disappear down a black hole; and for Peter to watch Jesus being taken, falsely tried and executed must have been horrendous.

The night had begun at the Last Supper. Peter would have found it difficult to understand the depth of meaning in Jesus' words and actions at that meal. Yet Jesus' 'new' Passover meal became the pattern for worship in the early church. The bread and the wine signified Jesus' blood and broken body – shed and given for our forgiveness and restoration. Peter may well have believed there was no hope of forgiveness after his denial, yet with Jesus there is always hope! Jesus was crucified, he carried our sin, and then he was mightily resurrected on Easter Day to conquer sin and death.

The Bible tells us that the consequence of sin is separation from God. Today, using the story of Peter, we will explain that we can be forgiven and know God as a special friend because of Jesus' death and resurrection.

3 Pray together

(If you have time and it is appropriate, you may wish to share communion together as a team.)

Pray that the teaching element today will come across clearly to the children.

Pray that the children will have a really great time today at *Seaside Rock*.

Ask for spiritual protection and safety across the whole holiday club.

Pray for strength, enthusiasm and gentleness for the team.

PRACTICAL PREPARATIONS

Talk through the morning's programme, and make sure everyone is aware of their responsibilities.

Encourage the team to be as welcoming and interactive with the children as possible. Encourage them to be firm in their discipline with the children, if necessary, and clear in their explanations of the teaching today.

Ensure that all resources are ready for the various activities.

Equipment checklist – Day 4

Security: registration forms, badges, pens, team lists.

Rock Groups: badges, pens, Bible, Rock Pool Challenge resources (flip chart paper, pens, pencils, large sticky notes and copies of Matthew 26:69–75), postcards ready to be taken home at the end of the session, spare paper.

Music: background CD and music for the *Seaside Rock* song.

Drama: costumes and props.

Technology: check PA, OHP, video projector etc are working and in focus, check acetates for songs, *Seaside Rock* logo acetate, Weather map and symbols, Beach Lookout, memory verse and Mega Question.

Activities: all equipment needed for games and craft.

Lifeguard: running order, notes, two T-shirts and a bag for the teaching application.

Refreshments: drinks and biscuits.

Teaching: Peter costume, bread and glass of wine, or *Seaside Rock* video ready to play in the right place.

ROCK POOL WELCOME
(10 minutes)
Rock Group time

Play some lively music on a CD player and put the *Seaside Rock* logo on the OHP to welcome the children as they arrive and are registered. They should join their Rock Groups. Any children bringing jokes or pictures for Lyn the Bin should place them in her special bin. If there's time, challenge the children to remember the memory verses from the last three days.

WELCOME TO THE SEASIDE!
(25 minutes)

LIFEGUARD WELCOME
The Lifeguard should end the Rock Group time and draw everyone's attention to the front. Welcome the children to Day 4 of *Seaside Rock*.

WEATHER FORECAST
Lifeguard: Hello, Heather on the Weather. Can you give us the weather for the beach today?

Heather: (*Bursting into the front of the room. The OHP with map is switched on by assistant.*) Indeed I can. Today is going to start with a bit of sun! (*Assistant puts sun pictures on screen.*) Before long

there will be some drizzle. (*Waterpistol.*) The rain is likely to get worse. (*More waterpistol.*) In fact, we could be looking at a snowstorm later on. (*A bucket of confetti, or something similar, over the head.*) By the evening, however, the sun will return – thank goodness! I'll be back tomorrow. Bye! (*Heather leaves in a rush.*)

Lifeguard: Thank you, Heather!

DANCING ON THE BEACH
Play a suitably bouncy piece of music with a couple of leaders leading the children in an aerobic workout. You could ask some children to come out and help lead the aerobics.

BEACH LOOKOUT
Explain the rules to the children, and play the game!

THEME SONG
Sing the theme song together.

PETER'S STORY – LIVE OR ON VIDEO
Either watch the fourth episode of the *Seaside Rock* video, or Peter arrives on stage to tell his story:

Peter should be suitably dressed and should be carrying some bread and a glass of wine.

Oh, hello! It's me again, Peter.

Have you ever really let someone down? Done something so bad that you think they'll never love you again, or never want to be your friend again? I have! And what made it even worse was that the person I really hurt was Jesus.

I'd been really good friends with Jesus for three years. I knew he was the Son of God and I'd seen him do amazing things. Then one night, Jesus called us together for a very special meal, called the Passover meal. As we all sat at the table, instead of saying the special words we usually say at the Passover meal, Jesus changed them. He took some bread and broke it. He gave it to us, and then said the bread was like his body, which was going to be broken for us. (*Physically tear the bread in front of the children.*) He then took some wine and gave it to us. He said that the wine was like his blood that was going to be poured out for our forgiveness. I didn't get it at the time. Body, blood, forgiveness… Then Jesus told us that he was about to be arrested and killed. He said that when it happened, we would all run away. That was absurd! I told him that I would never run away and leave him. But then Jesus said me that before the cockerel crowed (*Make cockerel sound.*) in the morning, I'd have said three times I didn't even know him. No way, I thought!

Anyway, Jesus *was* arrested… it was very frightening and really upsetting. You see Jesus had never, ever done anything wrong – he didn't deserve to be arrested, let alone killed. The soldiers took him to this house for a sort of trial. I followed at a distance. Just outside this house was a small fire. Several people were around the fire warming their hands, so I joined them, trying to keep an eye on what was happening to Jesus. As I waited, three different people asked me if I was one of Jesus' friends. I was frightened, and I told them all I didn't know who he was. I even said some really bad swear words.

And then the cockerel crowed, and I remembered what Jesus said – 'Before the cockerel crows, you'll say three times you don't know me.' I was so upset – I'd really let him down – that I ran away in floods of tears.

Jesus died that day on a wooden cross. He hadn't done anything wrong, but he died for you and me. Why? He told me at the meal – so we can be forgiven!

I needed to be forgiven, but I'll tell you all about what happened next tomorrow.

TEACHING APPLICATION

Props: two identical T-shirts, one spotless and the other one very mucky (pen marks, mud, coffee stains etc). Both should be kept in a bag which the children cannot see through.

(*Hold up the dirty T-shirt.*) Peter was like you and me. He did things wrong – he lied, said bad words, and hurt people just like we do. When we do those things, it makes our lives like this T-shirt – very mucky and dirty. When we are like this, we can't be friends with God because he's perfect.

Jesus died for us. He died to take the punishment for all the things we have done wrong. If you did something really bad at school, you would be punished for it. It's the same with our sins, the wrong things we do – God hates these things, and yet he loves us so much. But Jesus died to take our punishment, so that we can have our lives cleaned up. So if we say sorry, mean it and decide to follow Jesus, then it's like Jesus taking our muck, (*Put dirty T-shirt in the bag.*) washing us (*Give the T-shirts a whisk around in the bag.*) and pulling us out clean. (*Pull out perfect T-shirt.*) We'll find out more about that tomorrow. Now, because we are clean we can get to know Jesus as our greatest friend. Isn't that wonderful!

HOLIDAY SNAPSHOTS

Today's memory verse:

> If we confess our sins to God, he can always be trusted to forgive us and take our sins away.
> 1 John 1:9

First of all, read this from the Bible to show where it comes from. See pages 25 and 26 for some creative ideas on how to use memory verses, including information on the memory verse song, with accompanying actions, for each day. The words used in the memory verse song are a paraphrase.

ROCK POOL CHALLENGE
(10 minutes)

Gather the Rock Group around a piece of flip chart paper with a big cross pre-drawn on it. Ask the group if they understand why Jesus died on the cross and what it means for us.

Older children need to be encouraged that what they have been told is true. Give out Bibles or copies of Matthew 26. Invite some confident readers to read Matthew 26:69–75 with different children taking different parts. How did Peter let Jesus down? Could he ever be forgiven? Talk about the feelings this raises.

With younger children, read out these verses with as much expression as possible, encouraging the children to close their eyes and picture the scene. Then ask them to tell you the story with all the detail or act it out as a group.

Give the children an opportunity to respond to the teaching by handing out a large sticky note to each child. They can do several things with this. They can write a prayer to Jesus (some may be ready to ask for forgiveness and to commit themselves to following Jesus). Alternatively, they might want to write down or draw some of the things they know they have done wrong and then stick them on the cross as a way of saying sorry and thanking Jesus for dying, so that they can be forgiven. Some sensitivity will be needed here. Make sure that individual needs are met and that children are free to express their feelings.

REFRESHMENT KIOSK
(5 minutes)

Drinks as the children go to activities.

IN FOR A SWIM!
(25 minutes)

Beach Games and Beach Crafts (see page 42).

LET'S GO SUNBATHE!
(40 minutes)

Mega Question

Put today's Mega Question on the screen – 'What do these crosses mean?'

Ask some children for the answers, and finish by stating that when Jesus died on the cross, (*Point to Jesus' cross.*) he died for all the wrong in the world; (*Pointing to maths sum.*) he did it because he loves us so much (*Point to kiss.*) and now we have to make a choice, a bit like you do at a crossroads, about what we believe about Jesus. (*Point to the crossroads sign.*)

SONG

Either sing the *Seaside Rock* theme song or another suitable song. You could recap previous days' memory verse songs.

LYN THE BIN

Invite Lyn the Bin on to the stage. She should read out some jokes and show some pictures (chosen from those brought by the children), making witty, encouraging comments and awarding points. Lyn should encourage the children to bring in some jokes and pictures tomorrow. Remind the children that they should put their name and group on their piece of paper, and put them in Lyn's special bin when they arrive in the morning.

MEMORY JOGGER

Ask the children what they can remember of today's programme, including the memory verse.

DRAMA

See today's script on page 35.

CREATIVE PRAYER

Remind the children that God loves to hear our prayers. Tell them that as well as God loving to hear our words, he likes it when we use our bodies to praise him. Today we are going to clap and cheer God for all the wonderful things he has done!

> Dear Lord,
> Because you love us so much we want to give you a clap! (*Clap!*)
> Dear Lord,
> Because you died on a cross, so that we can be forgiven and become your friends, we want to give you a cheer! (*Cheer!*)
> Dear Lord,
> Because of the great time we've had today at *Seaside Rock* we give you a clap and a cheer! (*Clap and a cheer!*)
> Amen.

THEME SONG

Sing the theme song once more to bring an end to today's programme.

ROCK POOL GROUPS
(5 minutes)

Give the children today's postcard, and encourage them to complete the activities on it. They might like to bring it back tomorrow. Children should collect their belongings ready for departure. Make sure children are collected by the appropriate adult.

Memory verse:
If we confess our sins to God, he can always be trusted to forgive us and take our sins away.

1 John 1:9

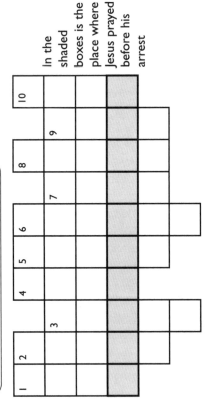

Seaside DAY 4 Rock

DAY 4'S MEGA CROSSWORD

In the shaded boxes is the place where Jesus prayed before his arrest

1. Written on the cross: _____ of the Jews
2. The number of times Peter said he didn't know Jesus
3. The main character in Seaside Rock
4 and 6. Jesus was tried in this man's home
5. Jesus was nailed to this
7. Jesus was buried here
8 and 9. Reminds us of Jesus' body and blood
10. Peter warmed himself by this

Think of something you have heard this week at *Seaside Rock* that puzzles you. Write it down here and make sure you ask someone about it.

Jesus' last meal with his friends, his trial and death on the cross were all part of today's story. We also heard how Peter let Jesus down. How could Jesus ever forgive him? Find out tomorrow!

Beach Lookout Day 4

Mega Question

What do these crosses mean?

I love you
xx

3 + 4 = 8 X

Day 5: The rock that lives

AIMS FOR THE DAY:

To tell the story of how Jesus forgave Peter and gave him a special job; to tell the children that Jesus is alive and wants us to follow him; to show that Jesus is the Rock that lives.

Peter: Peter tells us of Jesus' resurrection, and how Jesus forgave him on the beach. Peter relates Jesus' warning of persecution, and encourages us with his words in 1 Peter that Jesus is the Rock that lives!

Key story 1: Breakfast on the beach – John 21:1–19.

Key story 2: Peter's words about Jesus the living Rock – 1 Peter 2:4–8.

Key belief: Jesus is alive today and wants us to follow him, even when others think we are mad and pick on us!

TEAM PREPARATION

Spiritual preparation

Read together John 21:1–19 and 1 Peter 2:4–8.

1 Talk together

Briefly discuss these questions. (*Jot down your answers in two columns on a sheet of flipchart paper.*)

o   How did Peter feel after the crucifixion?

o   What does this beach story tell us about Jesus?

2 Share together

When Jesus appeared to the disciples after the resurrection, there was still unfinished business. In the story from John, we see Jesus lovingly and gently restoring Peter to his team. Peter had let Jesus down three times; Jesus gave him the opportunity to express his love three times. Then Jesus said to Peter, just like he did three years earlier when he sat in Peter's boat, 'Follow me'.

If anyone was qualified to teach about Jesus, it was Peter. In 1 Peter, he talks of Jesus as the 'precious foundation stone'. Peter tells us that Jesus will never disappoint anyone who trusts him.

Peter extends the concept of 'living stones' to talk about Jesus' followers. We have become 'living stones' and together we are the building that God wants – a temple, not of bricks and mortar, but of people's lives where God is active.

When Peter was forgiven by Jesus, he was also recommissioned to lead the fellowship of believers. Peter was given responsibility for caring for the fledgling church. Jesus also told Peter that he would soon face persecution. We know from Acts 12:1–19 that Peter was imprisoned – with God rescuing him on that occasion. Peter and the early church knew what it was like to be persecuted for their faith.

Today, we will challenge the children to follow Jesus, who is alive in heaven and here by his Holy Spirit. We will encourage them that even though living for Jesus can be tough, we have a living Rock on which we can build our lives.

3 Pray together

Praise Jesus for who he is, using the information above as your inspiration.

Pray that the children will understand that Jesus is alive and that he can help them to follow him by his Holy Spirit.

Pray that the children will have a really great time today at *Seaside Rock*.

Ask God to give you the opportunity to say something special to every child who comes today.

Pray for ongoing relationships with the children, and that they will respond well to the invitation to come to the *Seaside Rock* service on Sunday (or whatever follow-up session you are planning).

PRACTICAL PREPARATIONS

Talk through the morning's programme, and make sure everyone is aware of their responsibilities.

Encourage the team to use their knowledge of the children to meet their individual needs. Ask them to have a personal conversation with each of the children in their Rock Group.

Ensure that all resources are ready for the various activities.

Equipment checklist – Day 5

Security: registration forms, badges, pens, team lists.

Rock Groups: badges, pens, Bible, Rock Pool Challenge resources (flip chart paper, pens and Bibles or copies of John 21:15–19 and Matthew 26:69–75), postcards ready to be taken home at the end of the session, spare paper.

Music: background CD and music for the *Seaside Rock* song.

Drama: costumes and props.

Technology: check PA, OHP, video projector etc are working and in focus, check acetates for songs, *Seaside Rock* logo acetate, Weather map and symbols, Beach Lookout, memory verse, Mega Question and Creative Prayer.

Activities: all equipment needed for games and craft.

Lifeguard: running order, notes and a stick of rock for the teaching application.

Refreshments: drinks and biscuits.

Teaching: Peter costume, rock and fish, or *Seaside Rock* video ready to play in the right place.

ROCK POOL WELCOME
(10 minutes)

ROCK GROUP TIME

Play some lively music on a CD player and put the *Seaside Rock* logo on an OHP to welcome the children as they arrive and are registered. They should join their Rock Groups. Any children bringing jokes or pictures for Lyn the Bin should place them in her special bin. If there's time, challenge the children to remember the memory verses from the last four days.

WELCOME TO THE SEASIDE!
(25 minutes)

LIFEGUARD WELCOME

The Lifeguard should end the Rock Group time and draw everyone's attention to the front. Welcome the children to Day 5 of *Seaside Rock*. Go straight over to the weather forecast.

WEATHER FORECAST

Lifeguard: Hello, Heather on the Weather. Can you give us the weather for the beach today?

Heather: (*Bursting into the front of the room, with her suitcase ready for her forthcoming holiday. The OHP with map is switched on by assistant.*) Indeed I can. Oh what a wonderful day. The good news is that across Britain today, there will be sunshine! (*Assistant puts sun pictures on screen.*) In France, today there will be rain (*Waterpistol.*) In Russia, there will be snow. (*Confetti.*) In Germany there will be a severe hail storm. (*Bucket of ping-pong balls/small foam pieces/scrunched up bits of paper dropped on her head.*) And in Australia there will be a tornado. (*Fierce whistling sound and fan.*) Anyway, I'm off on holiday to the hotel at the end of the beach because it's so beautiful here! Bye! (*Heather leaves in a rush.*)

Lifeguard: Thank you, Heather!

DANCING ON THE BEACH

Using a suitably bouncy piece of music, a leader and children help lead the rest of the holiday club in an aerobic workout. Why not give these aerobics a final day feel, by acting out themes tackled in the previous days (eg nursing)? Keep it as energetic as possible!

BEACH LOOKOUT

Explain the rules to the children, and then play the game!

THEME SONG

Sing the theme song together.

PETER'S STORY – LIVE OR ON VIDEO

Either watch the fifth episode of the *Seaside Rock* video, or have Peter appear on stage to tell his story:

Peter should be suitably dressed and carrying a rock and a real fish if possible!

Oh, hello. It's me again – Peter.

Have you ever eaten fish for breakfast, cooked over a hot fire? Jesus cooked me some one day – on a very special day!

You know yesterday I told you about how I'd let Jesus down – by saying I didn't know him and by running away when he was arrested. I was supposed to be the leader of his followers, but I'd really mucked things up that day.

But a really amazing thing happened after Jesus died – he came back to life again! He was way too strong and powerful to let death win! Only a couple of days after he died on the cross, he came alive again. Some people thought we were making it up, but I saw him and I touched him — I knew he was alive!

And then there was that breakfast meal a week or so after Jesus had come back to life. We'd been fishing all night and caught nothing. Then this man on the beach shouted, 'Friends, throw your nets out on the other side of the boat.' We did, and our nets were suddenly miraculously full! The man turned out to be you-know-who — yep, Jesus! I jumped in the water and swam to him!

After the most delicious breakfast, Jesus did something so gentle and loving, I'll never forget it. You remember I said three times that I didn't even know him? Well, Jesus took me to one side and gently asked me three times if I really loved him. My answer was 'yes' each time, and I saw warmth and forgiveness in his eyes. He said, 'Peter, follow me!', and he also asked me to lead his people. Then lastly, Jesus went on to tell me about some things in the future. He warned me that I would be picked on and persecuted for my faith before going to be with him in heaven.

For about forty days after he had died and come back to life again, Jesus appeared to us and talked to us. Then we watched him go up into the sky into heaven. He was gone! A few weeks later he sent his Holy Spirit — God, to live in us, to give us the power to follow him!

Since that breakfast by the sea, I've followed Jesus, and led his people. It has been hard at times — some people hate our new message about following Jesus, and pick on us for telling them the good news. I've been put in prison, beaten up, rescued by angels and loads of other stuff. It's not always easy being a Christian, you know!

Anyway, I'd better go. One last thought… and it's a sort of 'Rocky' message. Remember my name, Peter, means Rock. If Jesus called me Rock, then I think he must be an even better rock… He's like a living Rock! He died, but he came back to life, and now he's alive in heaven. You can build your life on him. I wrote this bit in one of the two books I wrote — 'Come to Jesus Christ, he is the living stone.'

You can trust him. Keep following. Got to go! Bye!

TEACHING APPLICATION

Props: a stick of rock (CPO sell 'Jesus the Rock' rock — see inside back cover.)

This week we've got to know Peter. He was a bit of a big mouth to start with and often lost his temper. Jesus called Peter to follow, just like he calls you. I think Peter was like this stick of rock.

This stick of rock is colourful — full of all the fun of the seaside. Peter knew that although sometimes it is hard to be a Christian, Jesus adds colour and fun to life.

If you ate this rock it would be really tasty and full of flavour. Peter was changed by Jesus to be full of goodness, able to show Jesus' love to the world.

This stick of rock has got a name running through the middle — it says (*whatever the stick of rock you have says*). When Peter became a follower of Jesus, he started to live for him. It was like putting Jesus' name all the way though his life!

Do you remember the second verse of our theme song? That's what it's all about! (*Sing the second verse together.*)

HOLIDAY SNAPSHOTS

Today's memory verse:

> Come to Jesus Christ. He is the living stone that people have rejected, but which God has chosen and highly honoured.
> I Peter 2:4

First of all, read this from the Bible to show where it comes from. See pages 25 and 26 for some creative ideas on how to use memory verses, including information on the memory verse song, with appropriate actions, for each day. The words used in the memory verse song are a paraphrase.

ROCK POOL CHALLENGE
(10 minutes)

Gather each Rock Group around a piece of flip chart paper. Draw a huge stick of rock on the sheet with Jesus' name running through the middle of it. Ask the children to tell you why this is a picture of a Christian. Pick up on the points made by the Lifeguard in the teaching application.

With junior-aged children, give them a Bible or a copy of John 21:15–19 and Matthew 26:69–75. Draw six massive empty speech bubbles on flip chart paper — three on each side of a drawing of Peter. Write at the top of one side 'Fire' and the other side 'Beach'. Then ask a child to write down in the speech bubbles Peter's answers to the accusations at the fire in yesterday's story, and his answers to Jesus' questions on the beach. Reinforce John 21:19. Peter was going to suffer because he followed Jesus.

With younger children, tell them the answer to the question, 'Peter, do you love me?' is 'Yes I do.' Then read John 21:15–19, letting the children shout out the answer to Jesus' questions using these simple words (even though it is phrased slightly differently). Talk about the suffering Peter would face as he followed Jesus.

Complete the Rock Group Challenge by going back to the sheet of paper with the stick of rock. Ask the children to tell you everything they have discovered about Jesus and Peter. What did they do? What were they like? Record your answers on the sheet of flipchart paper.

You may also find it appropriate to spend some time discussing what other people think about Christians. Sometimes sticks of rock get broken – Christians can be picked on because of what they believe. Have the children encountered this? What should we do if people pick on us for what we believe or because we go to church?

REFRESHMENT KIOSK
(5 minutes)
Drinks as the children go to activities.

IN FOR A SWIM!
(25 minutes)
Beach Games and Beach Crafts (see page 42).

LET'S GO SUNBATHE!
(40 minutes)

MEGA QUESTION
Put today's Mega Question on the OHP – 'What did Peter mean when he said, "Jesus is the living Rock"?'

Ask a few children for answers to the Mega Question, reminding them of the story of the wise and foolish builders from Day 2. Jesus is living. He's alive today. If we hear what Jesus says and do it, we are building our lives on Jesus. So when difficult times come, we can trust someone big and strong and he will help us.

SONG
Sing the *Seaside Rock* theme song with great enthusiasm since this is the last day. You could put the previous days' memory verse songs together with today's song to complete the Memory Verse Medley. This is on the *Seaside Rock* CD. Alternatively you could use another song familiar to the children.

LYN THE BIN
Invite Lyn the Bin on to the stage. She should read out some jokes and show some pictures (chosen from those brought by the children), making witty, encouraging comments and awarding points. Lyn should thank all the children for their contributions to her bin during the week and maybe nominate the best contributions to receive a small prize.

MEMORY JOGGER
Ask the children what they can remember of today's programme, including the memory verse.

DRAMA
See today's script on page 38.

CREATIVE PRAYER
Encourage the children that knowing, following and learning about Jesus doesn't end here! The best way to follow Jesus is with other people's help, and as part of a group. Invite the children to come to your children's group/church/family service.

FINAL WORDS
To finish our *Seaside Rock* holiday club, it will be great to pray together. I have got a simple prayer here on the screen. (*Put up a copy of the following.*) Anyone can talk to God and he can hear everyone at the same time! (*Read the prayer to the children and then ask them all to stand and be ready to say it out loud to God as a final prayer, getting louder with each line.*)

> Thank you, Lord, for *Seaside Rock.*
>
> Thank you, Lord, for loving me.
>
> Thank you, Lord, that you forgive.
>
> Thank you, Lord, you're always there!
>
> Amen.

THEME SONG
Sing the theme song once more to bring an end to today's programme.

ROCK POOL GROUPS
(5 minutes)
Give the children today's postcard, and encourage them to complete the activities on it at home. Children should then collect their belongings ready for departure. Ensure they are collected by the appropriate adult.

DAY 5

Seaside Rock

Memory verse:
Come to Jesus Christ. He is the living stone that people have rejected but which God has chosen and highly honoured.

I Peter 2.4

Thank you for coming to *Seaside Rock!* We hope you've had a fantastic time and hope to see you again very soon! Write down here what has been the best thing about *Seaside Rock.*

Jesus forgave Peter and told him to tell others that Jesus is alive. Jesus wants everyone to know and love him. Peter found out that this is not always easy.

DAY 5'S MEGA MAZE

Can you help Peter swim to Jesus on the beach?

Beach Lookout Day 5

Mega Question

What did Peter mean when he said, "Jesus is the living Rock"?

FAMILY SERVICE OUTLINE B

AIM: To conclude the *Seaside Rock* programme; to encourage children and their families to consider what it means to trust Jesus.

Key story: Peter and John heal the lame man – Peter, the forgiven and empowered friend of Jesus, now becomes 'Jesus' to those he meets.

Key link to the holiday club: After the experience of meeting Jesus, Peter and John get on with the job of sharing their good news with others.

Key passage: Peter heals the lame beggar – Acts 3:1–10.

FEEDBACK: The Lifeguard should report back to the congregation on how the holiday club has gone. Relate how God has answered your prayers. Share the highs and the lows, and the challenges that you now face as a church. Particularly welcome the children and their families who have come to church for the first time today.

SONGS: Sing the *Seaside Rock* theme song together. You might like to give the children and the team the challenge of remembering the memory verses for the week. These can also be sung together.

DRAMA B: See the conclusion of the dramatic chase at the end of Episode 5! Reminisce with the characters on the key moments of the week (see page 39).

GAME: Beach Lookout. Play another version of this game. This time choose one of the acetates used during the week, so that those who came to *Seaside Rock* have a little advantage!

PRAYER: Praise God for the *Seaside Rock* holiday club. Ask the children what the high points have been and thank God for them. Ask God to bless all the children who came to the club throughout the week. Then pray about all the further opportunities there will be to follow up *Seaside Rock*.

READ: As you read Acts 3:1–10, ask a competent artist to draw the different movements of the characters on an OHP acetate(s). Alternatively, take six strips of stiff card and connect them together, end to end, with split pins. As the passage is read, make appropriate shapes such as a doorway shape, bent legs, straightened legs, outstretched arms. This will need practising!

CREATIVE PRAYER IDEA: Give each person in the room a sheet of A4 paper. Ask someone to demonstrate how to make a paper aeroplane. Ask the congregation to write their prayers onto the sheet of paper. Then together they should throw their planes around the church. Each person should pick up someone else's aeroplane and pray that prayer out loud altogether. Repeat as necessary!

TEACHING: Peter once walked on water (those using the video will have discovered this story). Peter was an ordinary man, who was able to do extraordinary things because of his faith and trust in Jesus. Today's story happened after Jesus had gone back to heaven. (You may need to fill in some of the details of the last weeks of Jesus' life.) Maybe Peter had similar feelings that the children and team have now that *Seaside Rock* is finished. Could Peter still live for Jesus, after Jesus had gone back to heaven? Can we follow Jesus as we go back to our homes and schools? Peter was filled with God's Spirit – God was living in him, to help him live for Jesus. The same is true for us if we follow Jesus. God will help us live for him. Peter needed to trust Jesus in today's story – trust him that he would heal the lame man. Peter healed the lame man in the name of Jesus – doing the things Jesus used to do. How excited Peter must have felt as he saw the lame man walking! Peter knew he couldn't lead the church without God's help and without putting all his trust in Jesus. He also needed God's help to be like Jesus to those around him. Challenge the congregation – are they willing to put all their trust in Jesus and to follow him with God's help?

WORSHIP: Choose some songs which the congregation know, and worship God together. You could sing the song 'Peter and John went to pray' (Junior Praise 198).

Other ways to use *Seaside Rock*

PART 8

FOLLOW-UP IDEAS

Seaside Rock doesn't have to finish at the end of one week! Here are a few ideas for follow-up:

o A midweek, after-school *Seaside Rock* club.

o A Saturday morning *Seaside Rock* club.

o A *Seaside Rock* beach party – an early evening event for all the family to enjoy. This could fit nicely on to the end of the *Seaside Rock* week.

o A series of church meetings based on the life of Peter.

o A small *Seaside Rock* cell group for those children who have shown particular interest and want to discover more. The *Y God?* course published by SU would be ideal for this. See inside front cover for details.

ADAPTING *SEASIDE ROCK* FOR A WEEKLY CLUB

A weekly club usually has the following limitations:

o Less time together.

o A smaller team.

o Less time to prepare.

o Less flexibility in preparing the venue.

A weekly club has the following benefits:

o Ongoing relationship-building with both children and families.

o Less time required in one particular week.

o Children who could not make a holiday club will be able to come.

o Leaders who are only available in the evenings/ on Saturdays can help.

Adapting the material

Here are a few guidelines on how to adapt one of the *Seaside Rock* daily outlines:

o Work out how much you can realistically fit in to the time available.

o Make sure you tell the story clearly (either with the video or having Peter appearing live).

o Allow time for children to unpack the story's meaning in smaller groups.

o There are many other Peter stories which could be used in a weekly club. Before you start, decide which other stories you will use and where they fit alongside the *Seaside Rock* stories.

A possible hour-long club programme:

o Welcome and group time/feedback from postcards	5 mins
o Prayer (led by Lifeguard)	1 min
o Dancing on the Beach	4 mins
o Beach Lookout	4 mins
o *Seaside Rock* drama	10 mins
o *Seaside Rock* theme song	3 mins
o Peter story – live or on video	5 mins
o Teaching/Rock Pool Challenge	12 mins
o Creative prayer	4 mins
o Game	11 mins
o Prayer to finish	1 min

EXTENDING SEASIDE ROCK TO TEN SESSIONS

Use the two family service outlines and the Peter stories.

The following stories are suggested to extend the programme.

Peter and Pentecost Acts 2

Peter discovered that once the Holy Spirit had come in place of Jesus, he had the courage and power to tell thousands of others about Jesus' life, death and resurrection. Identify with the children the key truths about Jesus that we would want to share.

Peter in prison Acts 12

Peter was arrested and miraculously rescued. The Holy Spirit is with us even in the most difficult times. Use this session to encourage children to stand firm in their faith.

Peter the old man 1 Peter 5

Peter as an old man wrote letters, assisted by Silas (5:12) to encourage and help other Christians. Making scrolls, what messages of encouragement can we write to others?

ADAPTING *SEASIDE ROCK* FOR USE WITH OTHER AGE-RANGES

Seaside Rock has been specifically written for use with children between the ages of five and eleven. However, you could adapt it for different age groups.

ADULTS: A whole series of adult talks can be put together following the development and ministry of Peter. You will find a list of the key stories of Peter's life on this page, from which a programme could be put together. This could also be used to prepare the church for the **Seaside Rock** week.

YOUTH: The **Seaside Rock** concept will not be easily accepted by fast growing teenagers. Teenagers can, however, learn a lot from Peter and a suitable youth programme built around his character would work well. Having someone gifted in drama impersonating Peter is a very powerful tool, and one that communicates well with young people. Another idea is to take the young people to a large lake or the seaside. Retelling the stories of Peter on the edge of some water, watching boats come and go, is a very powerful way to communicate.

PRE-SCHOOL: You could make some provision for pre-school children in your **Seaside Rock** week. Providing a room for mums with toddlers, with tea and coffee available, can make your club more inviting, and can give you the opportunity to develop relationships with the parents of the children who come. The **Seaside Rock** programme is not geared to children of this age. Although with some creativity anything is possible, bringing them into the main programme will change its nature, make things more difficult to run and may put some of the older children off coming.

However, the stories of Peter the fisherman, the family man and friend of Jesus are very appropriate to use with small children. The *Tiddlywinks* series of resource books, published by SU, will give you loads of ideas.

THE LIFE OF PETER

Peter was originally called Simon – a very common New Testament Jewish name. He was the son of Jonah and he had a younger brother called Andrew, who was the one who first introduced him to Jesus (John 1:40–42). He originally came from Bethsaida, on the eastern shore of the Sea of Galilee, where he was a fisherman. Simon would have been taught the Jewish Scriptures as a boy. He was a Galilean – Galileans had a reputation for an independence and energy that often got them into trouble. They were frank and open people. Simon was blunt, impetuous and straightforward. He would have spoken in a clear Galilean dialect and accent throughout his life. It even betrayed him as a follower of Christ when he stood around the fire according to Mark 14:70.

Simon was married before he became an apostle, and his wife's mother was healed by Jesus (Matthew 8:14). By the time of Jesus' ministry, Simon had settled at Capernaum. His house was large enough to give a home to his brother Andrew, his wife's mother, and also to Jesus, who may well have lived with him.

Andrew, a follower of John the Baptist, brought Simon to Jesus (John 1:41). Jesus recognised Simon at once, and declared that he would be called Cephas, an Aramaic name corresponding to the Greek *petros*, which means 'rock'. We next meet him by the Sea of Galilee (Matthew 4:18–22). There, the four fishing partners had shared an unsuccessful night's fishing. Jesus appeared suddenly, and entering into Simon's boat, told him to go out and let down the nets again. Simon did so and found his nets bursting with fish. On witnessing the miracle, he fell at Jesus' feet, crying, 'Go away from me, Lord, I am a sinful man!' (Luke 5:8). Jesus asked him to follow and become a 'fisher of people' (Matthew 4:19). Simon then began to take a more and more prominent part in the events of Jesus' life. He was the first to declare his faith in Jesus' Messiahship at Capernaum (John 6:66–69), and again at Caesarea Philippi (Matthew 16:13–20; Mark 8:27–30; Luke 9:18–20). This profession at Caesarea was one of great importance, and Jesus used these memorable words in response, 'You are Peter, and on this rock I will build my church.'

Peter was one of the three closest disciples to Jesus. He plays a major role in the following stories:

Peter walks on water (Matthew 14:22–33)

Peter rebukes Jesus for talking about suffering (Matthew 16:21–23)

Peter witnesses Jesus' transfiguration (Matthew 17:1–9)

Peter's taxes are paid using a coin from a fish's mouth (Matthew 17:24–27)

Peter prepares the Last Supper for Jesus (Luke 22:7–13)

Peter cuts off Malchus' ear as Jesus is arrested (Luke 22:47–51)

Peter denies he knows Jesus and deserts him (Matthew 26:69–75)

Peter is the first disciple to see the empty grave (John 20:1–10)

Peter is the first disciple to see Jesus alive (Luke 24:34; 1 Corinthians 15:5)

Peter is forgiven by Jesus at the breakfast on the beach (John 21:1–19)

Peter witnesses Jesus' ascension (Acts 1:6–11)

Peter preaches to three thousand people on the day of Pentecost (Acts 2:14–40).

By Pentecost, Jesus had moulded Peter into a new man. He was no longer the unreliable, self-confident man, swaying between rash courage and weak timidity, but the steadfast, trusted guide and leader of the early believers, a bold preacher for Christ in Jerusalem and abroad. He now lived up to his name of Cephas – the Rock! Peter's continuing story is recorded in these accounts:

Peter heals the man at the temple gates and is persecuted (Acts 3,4)

Peter preaches to the Jewish Council (Acts 5:29–32)

Peter goes on a missionary journey to Lydda and Joppa (Acts 9:32–43)

Peter takes the Christian faith to Cornelius, a Gentile (Acts 10)

Peter miraculously escapes from prison (Acts 12:1–19)

Peter speaks at the Christian council in Jerusalem regarding Gentile believers (Acts 15:1–31; Galatians 2:1–10)

We have no further mention of Peter in the book of Acts. He seems to have gone to Antioch after the council at Jerusalem, where he encountered Paul (Galatians 2:11–16).

Peter writes two books (1 and 2 Peter)

After this, he appears to have carried the gospel to the west, and ended up in Rome (1 Peter 5:13, where 'Babylon' refers to Rome). Church tradition states that he was crucified in Rome, possibly upside down, about AD 65.

ORDERING  RESOURCES

To order any of the resources recommended in this book from Mail Order, complete this form.
The books should also be available from a local Christian bookshop.

ISBN	Title	Quantity	Price (each)	

When ordering, please include ISBN, title, quantity and price.

All titles subject to availability.

Prices subject to change without notice.

TOTAL COST OF GOODS	
Postage & packing	
Donation to Scripture Union	
Total Enclosed	

ORDERING INFORMATION

Please complete the payment details below.

All orders must be accompanied by the appropriate payment.

Send this completed form to:

Scripture Union Mail Order
PO Box 5148
Milton Keynes MLO, MK2 2YX
Tel: 01908 856006 Fax: 01908 856020

ORDER VALUE	UK	EUROPE	REST OF WORLD	AIR MAIL
Under £6.00	£1.25	£2.25	£2.25	£3.50
£6.00 to £9.99	£2.25	£3.50	£4.50	£6.00
£10.00 to £14.99	Free of charge	£3.50	£4.50	£6.00
£15.00 to £29.99	Free of charge	£5.50	£5.50	£11.00
£30.00 to £49.99	Free of charge	18% of order value	20% of order value	Price on request
£50.00 to £100.00	Free of charge	18% of order value	20% of order value	Price on request
£100.00 and over	Free of charge	18% of order value	20% of order value	Price on request

ORDERED BY

Mrs/Mr/Miss/Ms/Rev _____

Address _____

_____

_____

Postcode _____

Daytime tel _____

(for any query about your order)

DELIVERY ADDRESS (if different)

Mrs/Mr/Miss/Ms/Rev _____

Address _____

_____

_____

Postcode _____

Daytime tel _____

(for any query about your order)

PAYMENT DETAILS

Method of Payment ☐ Cheque* ☐ Mastercard ☐ Visa ☐ Switch ☐ Postal order*

Credit card number: ☐☐☐☐ ☐☐☐☐ ☐☐☐☐   Expiry date: ☐☐☐☐

Switch card number: ☐☐☐☐☐☐☐☐☐☐☐☐   Expiry date: ☐☐☐☐

Issue number of switch card: ☐☐☐

Signature: _____   Date: _____

(necessary if payment by credit card)   *made payable to Scripture Union

Please print name which appears on credit card: _____

Please print the address the card is billed to, if different from above: _____

To be included on SU's supporters database and receive our quarterly SU News and other mailings please tick this box ☐